CELEBRATE
1OO YEARS OF
GREAT TASTE

THE 1OOTH-ANNIVERSARY
EDITION COOKBOOK

NeimanMarcus

NEIMAN MARCUS TASTE

Karen Katz
2017

NEIMAN MARCUS TASTE

TIMELESS AMERICAN RECIPES

Kevin Garvin with John Harrisson

PHOTOGRAPHS BY ELLEN SILVERMAN

Clarkson Potter/Publishers
New York

Library of Congress Cataloging-in-Publication Data
Garvin, Kevin, 1958–
    Neiman Marcus taste: timeless American recipes / Kevin Garvin with
John Harrisson. — 1st ed.
    Includes index.
ISBN 978-0-307-39435-4
1. Cookery.   I. Harrisson, John.   II. Neiman Marcus.   III. Title.
TX714.G3659   2007
641.5—dc22   2007010071

Printed in Japan

Home decor and tabletop accessories available at Neiman Marcus and Bergdorf
Goodman. Grateful acknowledgment is also made to the following vendors,
whose products appear in this book's photographs: Match, William Yeoward,
Bernardaud, ABH Design, and Lori Weitzner Design.

10 9 8 7 6 5 4 3 2 1

First Edition

To the cooks who have come before
and created timeless recipes,
to all of our guests and home cooks
everywhere who appreciate fine food,
and to those who will follow
in our footsteps.

CONTENTS

PREFACE People ask all the time how I got interested in cooking, and I always answer, "My mom was a great cook." Mealtime was at the center of our family life, and seven nights a week we gathered around the dinner table to eat together. We usually started with a green salad, followed by a main course of meat, fish, or poultry accompanied by a fresh vegetable and a starch. Dessert was either Jell-O or pudding or a cake Mom had made that day. Mom started most of her dishes by browning an onion or sautéing some garlic, then searing a piece of meat in the perfumed oil. As I observed this process, the sounds and sights of cooking became just as alluring to me as the smells; before long, I wanted to help create the meal. Soon, I was the one responsible for the fabulous smells permeating our home. One of my favorite meals, growing up, was a Sunday roast pork dinner with Brussels sprouts—a combination I still love. You'll find this recipe on page 177.

At the age of fourteen, I got my first job, at Piccolo's Pizza, not far from where I grew up in the northeast section of Philadelphia. Danny Nejberger and Tony Foster were great bosses who soon had me working as a utility person; I did most of the jobs in the kitchen, from peeling onions to grating cheese and slicing hoagie rolls. It could have seemed tedious or menial, but I loved it. I realized I had a certain talent for organization, and no matter what task was placed in front of me, I gave it 100 percent and always tried to do my very best. I soon found that this effort would be rewarded either with praise or sometimes a little extra money in my paycheck—not a bad lesson to learn when getting started in the business world.

Years later, as I look back on this first job, I realize I came to love this business so much because I worked with great people and I was having fun. Had my first experience not been as enjoyable, I probably would have left the kitchen in search of a different career. To this day, I tell our cooks it is important to have a passion for the profession, to love the kitchen, and to have fun in order to succeed as a chef. While my job today as vice president and culinary director of Neiman Marcus is a bit more demanding than my responsibilities at Piccolo's, there is nothing in the world I would rather be doing.

L'ESCRITEAU

Menu from a 1957 Chevaliers du Tastevin dinner in the Zodiac Restaurant

RECEPTION

On Boira:

Apéritif Bourguignon
(Chablis et Cassis)

Le Feuilleté Jurassien

PREMIÈRE ASSIETTE

La Bisque de Homard aux Quenelles

DEUXIÈME ASSIETTE

On Boira:

Montrachet 1955
Marquis de la Guiche

Le Suprême de Turbot aux Raisins
de Muscat

TROISIÈME ASSIETTE

On Boira:

Chanson Beaune
Clos de Feves 1952

Le Salmis de Pintadeau au
Chambertin

POUR SE RAFFRAICHIR

Le Granité Dom Pérignon

QUATRIÈME ASSIETTE

On Boira:

Chambertin Armand Rousseaux
en Magnum 1949

Le Filet de Boeuf à la
Façon des Ducs de Bourgogne

La Salade Néva

ISSUE DE TABLE

On Boira:

Armand Roux
Richebourg 1949

Le Plateau de Fromages

BOUTEHORS

On Boira:

Dom Pérignon 1947

Le Biscuit Glaçé Inédit
Les Petits Fours Champs Elysées

On Dégustera

Marc de Bourgogne
Chartreuse 1944

Café Noir

La Corbeille de Fruits

Le Maître des Cuisines
ANDRE PAPION
Sommelier ROBERT GOURDIN
Décors de table par JANE COLE
Cristaux de BACCARAT
Porcelaines de WEDGWOOD

Pour l' Initiation

Clos de Vougeot
Grand Maupertuis 1945

Apres Les Ceremonies

On Servira
Dom Pérignon 1947

INTRODUCTION As Neiman Marcus celebrates its one-hundredth anniversary, with more than fifty years of fabulous meals behind us, this is the perfect time to share some of our classic, timeless recipes with our longtime customers and new friends alike. After all, food at Neiman Marcus has a rich and delicious history. When I traveled around the country promoting our first book, the *Neiman Marcus Cookbook,* I had a chance to meet and talk with our customers to learn what dishes they enjoyed most at our restaurants and what interested them most about our history. Our customers told me which recipes they wanted as well as the style of cooking they prefer.

I heard over and over again that our customers want to re-create at home their favorite Sunday supper-style dishes, from Potato and Bacon Soup and White Cheddar Cheese Soufflé to Stuffed Flounder with Deviled Crab and Roasted Shoulder of Pork. I have tried to accommodate the personal feedback I received in this cookbook, which is a collection of more than a hundred recipes. Among them are those we are asked to part with year in and year out, all perfect for memorable meals to be shared with family and friends. Many of the book's recipes were created decades ago and remain beloved today, and others are newer favorites that are sure to tempt for years to come. At the end of each recipe you'll find a Simplicity key. One-star recipes are simplest in terms of effort and skill; five-star recipes require extra time to prepare and/or more advanced culinary skills.

The affinity between our customers and our food service dates to 1953, when we opened our first restaurant, the Zodiac. To delve into the history of our food service operation is to pay homage first and foremost to Helen Corbitt, the initial director of restaurants at Neiman Marcus. Much has been written about Helen, the feisty grand dame of Texas cooking, and this book is, in large part, a celebration of her contribution to the culinary world. Neiman Marcus remains indebted to Helen for establishing a high level of excellence for our restaurants in every way—imaginative food, impeccable service, and a memorable dining experience. We honor her innovations by creating modern versions of her masterpiece recipes.

Visiting Dallas a few years ago to launch her latest cookbook, Julia Child came to the Zodiac at the Neiman Marcus store for lunch. I had the good fortune to sit across from her at the table. Julia talked almost exclusively about Helen Corbitt, and she enjoyed the anecdotes I shared about her. Julia regretted that the two of them had never met because she believed Helen was one of the very first chefs in the United States to identify modern American cooking. It was during this lunch with Julia Child that I realized just how influential Helen was in creating American cuisine.

Stanley Marcus ("Mr. Stanley"), a gourmet in his own right, recognized Helen Corbitt as a unique talent. In 1955, two years after the Zodiac opened in the Dallas store, he persuaded her to join Neiman Marcus to run the restaurant. Described by contemporary writers as a "brash transplanted Yankee firebrand" and a creative cook who "waged her own revolution on the naive palates of hungry Texans," Helen spent the next fifteen years firmly establishing Neiman Marcus as an innovative force on the American culinary scene. James Beard, the dean of American cuisine, was one of her admirers; he called her "the queen of the ladies' lunch." Food writer Earl Wilson described her as the best cook in Texas. For years, her ever-popular recipes made our store a food destination for haute cuisine, and all these years later, some of her creations—the orange soufflé, the popovers with strawberry butter, the chicken salad—can still be found in our repertoire, even if they are updated or adapted a little.

Helen Corbitt was born in Benson Mines, in upstate New York, in 1906 to a prosperous Irish-American family. She learned baking, dessert-making, and artistic food presentation from her mother, and when she was just seven years old, she baked her first pound cake. After earning a bachelor's degree in home economics from Skidmore College, Helen had ambitions to become a doctor. However, the Depression put paid to those plans, and instead she trained as a therapeutic dietician at Presbyterian Hospital in Newark, New Jersey. She moved on as an intern at the Cornell Medical Center in New York City, where she gained a reputation as an innovator.

Helen sought to widen her horizons, but the times were tough. The only viable position she was offered was teaching large-scale cooking and management at the University of Texas in Austin. Her initial reaction was less than positive: "I said, 'Who the hell wants to go to Texas?' Only I didn't say *hell* in those days. I learned to swear in Texas." Although she was often tempted to return to the relative civilization of New York, as she saw it, she instead accepted a position managing the food service at the swanky Houston Country Club, in part because she was penniless. As the years went by, Helen reconciled herself to the way of doing things in the Lone Star State and adopted it as her home.

Helen was detail-oriented and exacting. Her hands-on style brought success and a measure of fame. She was recruited by Joske's department store in Houston to manage the Garden Room, a popular tearoom, and she combined this appointment with establishing her own catering business. It was at Joske's that Helen served the Duke of Windsor, the former King Edward VIII of England, who asked her how she made the avocado mousse she served him. Helen later named a menu staple after him—the Duke of Windsor sandwich, still a bestseller. But it wasn't long before Helen returned to Austin to work at the Driskill Hotel, an institution frequented by the Texas political and social elite. During this period she established what became a longtime friendship with Lyndon B. Johnson, who later tried, unsuccessfully, to lure her to Washington, D.C., to preside over the White House kitchen.

Stanley Marcus told me it took him several years of ardent pursuit before Helen Corbitt finally agreed to work for him. Mr. Stanley sent her flowers every few months to demonstrate his seriousness in wanting her to be the Neiman Marcus food director. He sent her flowers for over a year until one day, having had her fill of Austin, Helen called Mr. Stanley to ask when she could start. Trying his best to conceal his delight and excitement, he told her the next Monday would be good. Helen hit the ground running, and the crowds were soon lined up outside the Zodiac.

Mr. Stanley knew of her temperamental, no-nonsense reputation; "my wild Irish genius" is how he affectionately described the redheaded Corbitt. If he wanted to ask her a business question, he would often step into the kitchen and listen carefully before proceeding to be sure Helen was not having one of her legendary spells of temper. One of the qualities Mr. Stanley most admired in Helen was her dedication; she was always in the kitchen, directing, looking at everything that went out to the dining room, and creating new dishes. She authored five bestselling cookbooks; her first, *Helen Corbitt's Cookbook,* published in 1957, has been reprinted more than thirty times and has sold more than 350,000 copies. Anthologies of her recipes have also been produced, and she even edited a cookbook on Mexican food. In 1961, Helen became the first woman in the United States to receive the Golden Plate Award, the food service industry's highest honor. She received many other awards and accolades over the years, and she was particularly proud to be named among the ten most influential women in Texas.

In the 1950s, Neiman Marcus became famous for "Fortnight," an annual two-week celebration that focused on a particular country or region. During these events, the store, including the Zodiac, was decorated appropriately. Helen would adapt the menu and, sometimes, guest chefs and their teams were brought in from the highlighted country to prepare special dinners. In *The Best from Helen Corbitt's Kitchens,* Patty V. MacDonald describes the Zodiac in Helen's years as "an oasis for daytime glamour. Dallas citizens and out-of-town visitors could enjoy a noonday feast along with a display of the latest fashions worn by sleek, slim Neiman Marcus models. . . . Before long, affluent Texans began driving miles into town to wait in long lines for a Corbitt meal. Not only Texans, but every visiting celebrity that came through Dallas vied for a seat in the Zodiac Room."

Mr. Stanley sent Helen globe-trotting so she could bring back ideas and the latest trends in food, and she did not disappoint him. Helen opened the first Mariposa restaurant when Neiman Marcus opened its store in Houston, supervising an imaginative and stylish menu with continental overtones. She often held cooking classes for Neiman Marcus customers, and these were always so popular that they were sold out well in advance. Helen continued as a consultant to Neiman Marcus after her official retirement, and even supervised the opening of the first Neiman Marcus restaurants outside Texas when the company established stores in Bal Harbour, Florida, and in Atlanta. Helen was ready to acknowledge that her success over the years was due, in part, to the leeway Mr. Stanley gave her to mastermind the menu and make decisions on restaurant service and interior design.

Although she never married, Helen had a keen eye for the men. In fact, she dedicated one of her books, *The Helen Corbitt Cookbook,* to the men in her life. As she wrote, "Anyhow, I say 'I love men'—tall ones, short ones, old ones,

young ones, fat ones, thin ones. All! All the ones who eat. And they all eat." Helen was nothing if not inclusive! To this day, men come up and tell me how much they enjoyed her men-only cooking classes; she could cuss and drink with the best of them while creating some of the best recipes her students had ever tried. These colorful stories helped inspire me to start my own cooking school at Neiman Marcus. I think Helen would be proud of our school and the classroom space we created in our downtown Dallas store.

Without doubt, Helen Corbitt was ahead of her time—sometimes, she was *way* ahead. People in the city old enough to remember those days still mention her with admiration and affection. Without her, I very much doubt that Neiman Marcus would have gained the reputation in the culinary world that it has. Helen Corbitt occupies a privileged place in the pantheon of Neiman Marcus greats. She died in 1978, and, truly, this book is a testament to her continuing legacy.

The legacy of Helen Corbitt did not end when she retired. When I first started at Neiman Marcus in the 1990s, every kitchen in the company owned a well-used copy of *The Helen Corbitt Cookbook*. Many of our restaurants continued to serve her original Chicken Velvet Soup, Chicken Curry, and Pecan Ball recipes. My first impulse was to change things radically—after all, it was now the 1990s—but I soon realized that adapting and updating her classic recipes was the smarter way to go. She was farsighted; well before it became the norm, she advocated the use of seasonal ingredients, cooking with fresh fruits and vegetables only, and she was adamant that the food prepared in the store restaurants be made in small

quantities. She gained a reputation for her culinary artistry as well as her knack for organizing unique parties and special events with great style and gusto. These traditions live on today at Neiman Marcus.

Another thing that remains is Helen's collection of index card files, which contain hundreds and hundreds of recipes. Together with her cookbooks, these formed the nucleus of information I sifted through carefully to select the recipes and themes for this cookbook. I realized anew what a creative cook she was, and what a consummate party-giver. The jacket copy for one of her cookbooks informs the reader, "If you are planning a party, Helen Corbitt's advice will eliminate hysteria and backache. She is an experimenter, a resourceful kitchen magician." In another book, she writes, "In these days of shortcuts, mixes, and packaged meals, I hope you will forgive my taking you back to the kitchen." Those words are just as applicable today, if not more so.

This book, then, takes us back to the kitchen, where we revive some old favorites of Helen's, dress up others, and add in a few of my own for good measure. These recipes reflect the way we cook and eat, and I have no doubt most of them will still be cherished and enjoyed for decades to come. That is the best way I know to celebrate an extraordinary—and extraordinarily successful—one hundred years.

1921 — FIRST MISS AMERICA PAGEANT

1922 — LINCOLN MEMORIAL IS DEDICATED IN WASHINGTON D.C.

RIN TIN TIN FILMS FIRST

1953 — MARILYN MONROE STARS IN "GENTLEMEN PREFER BLONDES"

1954 — BOOK "LORD OF THE FLIES" IS RELEASED

GUNSM

breads and morning pastries

BAKING CLASS at the Culinary Institute of America remains a vivid memory for me. While most of the students were still fast asleep, the baking students rose at 4:00 A.M. and headed to the bakery to get ready for breakfast. I remember this class so well because I took it in the middle of the winter, and that time of the morning in that season up on the Hudson River in Hyde Park, New York, is distinctly chilly! That made the contrast of emerging from the bitter cold into a warm, well-lit bakery rich with the smell of rising yeast and the heat from the huge ovens warming you up all the more memorable and wonderful. This is probably when I realized I was truly a morning person.

We would never have considered our instructor, Chef Bradley, a scientist, yet the skill this man possessed in bread-making made him a master at what he did. Bread baking has come a long way in the

United States in the past fifty years. In Philadelphia, we were spoiled with great bread, but if you ventured too far from the East or West Coast, you were hard pressed to find any good bread at all. Most of the country was the land of Wonder Bread. Then, in the early 1980s, bakers joined the great food revolution taking hold across the nation. The term *artisan baker* joined the culinary lexicon, and today, most cities boast great breads made locally—due, in part, to a critical mass of young chefs, many trained in culinary schools, who fell in love with the art and science of baking and the production of fine breads. Chef Bradley would be proud!

From the early Helen Corbitt days, the bakery at Neiman Marcus was an important part of the overall food program. At the beginning of the 1970s, the bakery became too small for the needs of our three Dallas-area stores, and an expanded space was created on Haskell Street, where the bakery stayed well into the 1980s. Today, the downtown store has reopened the bakery in the Zodiac kitchen and turns out customer favorites every day. In this chapter, we combine breakfast baked items with savory recipes to give you a wide variety of fresh homemade baked goods à la Neiman Marcus. Many of the recipes have been classics for years, and I believe all of them will continue to stand the test of time.

GARLIC AND HERB MONKEY BREAD

Monkey Bread has been a signature item at Neiman Marcus for years, and it remains as popular as ever. There's nothing quite like the smell of yeast bread proofing under a damp cloth in a warm spot in your kitchen. Even better, when this bread hits the oven, the aromas of the herbs and garlic waft enticingly. Before you know it, your guests will be begging to know where the delicious smells are coming from. Don't let them get at the bread before dinner is served, or you'll have nothing left!

1 cup milk

1 tablespoon plus 1 teaspoon active dry yeast
(1½ packages)

¼ cup sugar

1 teaspoon kosher salt

1 cup (2 sticks) unsalted butter, melted, plus
additional butter for the loaf pan

¼ cup Roasted Garlic Purée (page 276)

1 teaspoon freshly cracked black pepper

1 teaspoon minced fresh rosemary

1 teaspoon minced fresh thyme

1 teaspoon minced fresh parsley

1 teaspoon minced fresh chives

3¼ cups all-purpose flour, sifted

Pour the milk into a saucepan and set over medium heat for 2 to 3 minutes, or until lukewarm (but not hot), about 110°F. Transfer the warm milk to the bowl of an electric mixer fitted with a paddle attachment (alternatively, the dough can be mixed by hand in a large bowl). Add the yeast and a pinch of the sugar and let stand for about 5 minutes, until the yeast is dissolved. Add the remaining sugar, the salt, and ½ cup of the melted butter. Add the roasted garlic, pepper, and fresh herbs and, with the mixer running on low speed, slowly add the flour, mixing for 2 or 3 minutes, until a soft dough forms. Transfer the dough to a lightly oiled bowl, turn the dough to coat, and cover with plastic wrap. Let rise in a warm place for about 1 hour, or until doubled in volume.

Preheat the oven to 350°F. Butter a loaf pan (preferably measuring 8 by 4 by 2 inches).

Punch down the dough and turn out onto a lightly floured work surface. Using your fingertips, spread the dough to a ¼-inch thickness. Place the remaining ½ cup melted butter in a shallow bowl. With a pizza cutter or a sharp knife, cut the dough into 1 by 2-inch pieces. Dip each piece of dough into the melted butter and arrange upright (long side up) in the prepared loaf pan. Start by leaning the pieces up against one end of the pan and then continue nestling the strips together so they support and abut one another. Let rise in a warm place, covered with a damp towel, for 20 to 30 minutes, or until the dough reaches the top of the loaf pan. Transfer to the oven and bake for about 20 minutes, or until golden brown. Brush the top again with any leftover butter.

CHEF'S NOTE: This bread freezes well after baking. Defrost slowly and heat in a 325°F oven for 10 to 15 minutes, until hot and crusty.

YIELD: 1 LOAF

SIMPLICITY: + +

SAVORY PARMESAN POPOVERS

Popovers are a perennial favorite at Neiman Marcus restaurants, and our tradition is to serve them with strawberry butter (you can find that combination in our **Neiman Marcus Cookbook***). This savory version is enhanced by the addition of cheese, herbs, and butter, but if you want to make plain popovers, simply omit the final three ingredients listed and use the same method. Serve with any main course (they are paired in this book with Chicken à la King on page 155) or to accompany Brie or baked Camembert cheese. The aroma while they are baking is to die for.*

3½ cups milk

4 cups all-purpose flour

1½ teaspoons kosher salt

1 teaspoon baking powder

6 large eggs, at room temperature

1½ cups grated Parmesan cheese

¼ cup dried mixed herbs, such as parsley, thyme, and rosemary

4 tablespoons (½ stick) unsalted butter, cut into 12 pieces

Preheat the oven to 450°F.

Pour the milk into a saucepan and set over medium heat for 2 to 3 minutes, or until lukewarm (but not hot), about 110°F. Sift together the flour, salt, and baking powder into a large bowl. In the bowl of an electric mixer fitted with a wire whisk, beat the eggs on low speed for about 3 minutes, until foamy and pale in color. Stir in the warm milk and continue to mix at low speed. Gradually add the flour mixture to the beaten eggs at low speed, then increase the speed to medium and mix for 2 minutes longer. Let the batter rest for 1 hour at room temperature.

Spray a 12-cup nonstick popover tin generously with nonstick spray and set on a baking sheet. Fill the cups of the tin almost to the top with batter. Sprinkle the cheese and dried herbs evenly over the top of the batter and add a piece of butter. Bake for 15 minutes, then reduce the oven temperature to 375°F. Bake the popovers for 30 to 35 minutes longer, or until they are deep golden brown and crispy on the outside and airy on the inside.

CHEF'S NOTE: These popovers must be made in a nonstick popover pan, which you can find at specialty kitchenware stores such as Williams-Sonoma and Sur La Table.

YIELD: 12 POPOVERS

SIMPLICITY: +

TEXAS CORN BREAD
with Caramelized Onions

This recipe is a nod to our Texas roots. It's more than just a corn bread—it's almost a meal in itself, and ideal for Texas-size appetites! At Neiman Marcus, we serve it with Venison Chili (page 179), but it is the perfect accompaniment to any stew.

2 bacon slices, diced

1 small white onion, minced

1 cup fresh corn kernels (from 1 large ear of corn)

2 cups all-purpose flour

1 cup yellow cornmeal

2½ teaspoons baking powder

2 teaspoons kosher salt

1½ cups milk

2 large eggs

8 tablespoons (1 stick) unsalted butter, melted

2 teaspoons sliced fresh chives

1 teaspoon coarsely ground black pepper

1 teaspoon barbecue spice mix, such as Paul Prudhomme

Preheat the oven to 400°F.

Set a sauté pan over medium-high heat and add the bacon. Cook for 3 minutes, stirring often, then add the onion. Continue cooking for 6 to 8 minutes, until the onion is browned and caramelized. Add the corn and cook for 3 minutes longer. Remove from the heat and let cool slightly. Meanwhile, place a heavy 9-inch cast-iron skillet in the oven for at least 5 minutes and let it get very hot. (Alternatively, use a round 9-inch cake pan sprayed with nonstick spray.)

In a bowl, mix together the flour, cornmeal, baking powder, and salt. Whisk in the milk, eggs, and 7 tablespoons of the melted butter and mix thoroughly. Fold in the bacon-corn mixture, chives, and pepper.

Carefully remove the hot skillet from the oven and add the remaining 1 tablespoon butter, swirling to coat the surface. Pour in the batter and sprinkle with the barbecue spice. Bake for 15 to 20 minutes, until firm, golden brown, and a toothpick inserted in the center comes out clean. Serve warm.

CHEF'S NOTES: This corn bread can be refrigerated and reheated later. If you double this recipe and substitute it for the French bread in the turkey stuffing (see page 138), you'll have a great corn-bread dressing recipe for the holidays. The addition of the corn and bacon really jazzes it up!

YIELD: ONE 9-INCH SKILLET (SERVES 8 TO 12)

SIMPLICITY: + + +

SAVORY PRETZEL STICKS
with Caraway

Helen Corbitt started making these savory sticks for parties, and they were soon much sought-after at Neiman Marcus events during the 1950s and '60s. They are definitely ripe for revival during our one-hundredth anniversary. They make a terrific savory accompaniment to soups and a great cocktail snack. We also crisscross these bread sticks on top of salads as a garnish.

Garlic and Herb Monkey Bread (page 24)

2 large eggs, beaten

4 tablespoons kosher salt

4 tablespoons caraway seeds

Prepare the Monkey Bread dough and let rise for 1 hour, or until doubled in volume. Punch down the dough and turn out onto a lightly floured work surface. Using your fingertips, spread the dough to a ¼-inch thickness. Cut the dough into 25 to 30 1-inch squares and then form the squares into round balls. Set the balls about 1 inch apart on a clean work surface, cover with a damp towel, and let rise for about 30 minutes. With your fingertips, press a ball into a roughly triangular shape, about ⅛ inch thick (each side of the triangle should be 3 to 4 inches long). Set a triangle on a lightly floured work surface, brush with the beaten eggs, and sprinkle with about ⅛ teaspoon each of the salt and caraway seeds. Roll up the triangle and use your fingers to gently twist and elongate the rolled dough into a compact twist 5 to 6 inches long. Set on a baking sheet lined with parchment paper. Repeat with the remaining dough squares, setting them 2 inches apart on the sheet. Brush again with the egg wash and sprinkle with the salt and caraway seeds. Cover the dough with a damp towel and let rise in a warm place for about 30 minutes, or until the sticks have doubled in volume.

Meanwhile, preheat the oven to 350°F.

Remove the towel and bake the bread sticks for about 30 minutes, or until golden brown.

CHEF'S NOTE: There are many types of coarse salt on the market now to choose from. Get creative and try different kinds; this recipe is a perfect way to taste-test them and develop your own favorites.

YIELD: 25 TO 30 STICKS

SIMPLICITY: + + +

BUBBIE HIRSCH'S CHALLAH

Challah is an attractively braided leavened bread made with eggs and traditionally served on the Jewish Sabbath. Its soft, rich, and airy texture is similar to that of brioche. It has a subtle sweetness and is tremendously versatile; it makes great sandwiches and French toast, and there's simply nothing better if you enjoy a good grilled cheese sandwich. This recipe comes from Bubbie Hirsch, the mother of Anita Hirsch, corporate chef and my right-hand person in the kitchen at Neiman Marcus. Bubbie is the Yiddish word for grandmother, and back in the day, Bubbie Hirsch was also one of those supermoms—a great cook with an innovative kosher repertoire enjoyed by her family (which included five children and husband, Lou). In addition, she managed a full-time secretarial job. Sometimes she made unbraided mini-loaves of this Sabbath bread for sandwiches.

1 tablespoon plus 1 teaspoon active dry yeast
  (1½ packages)

5 tablespoons sugar

1¼ cups warm water

4½ cups all-purpose flour

½ tablespoon kosher salt

¼ cup vegetable oil

3 large eggs

1 tablespoon poppy seeds (optional)

In the bowl of an electric mixer fitted with a paddle attachment, mix together the yeast, 1 tablespoon of the sugar, the water, 1¼ cups of the flour, the salt, and the oil. Mix on low speed for 1 minute. (Alternatively, the dough can be mixed by hand in a large bowl.) Add 2 of the eggs, the remaining 4 tablespoons sugar, and half of the remaining flour and mix until incorporated. Add the rest of the flour and mix on medium speed for 4 minutes; if the dough is too wet, add a little more flour until the dough no longer sticks to the sides of the bowl. Remove the dough from the mixing bowl and place in a lightly oiled large bowl. Cover with a slightly damp towel and let rise in a warm place for 2½ hours.

Preheat the oven to 350°F. Lightly butter a 12-inch baking sheet.

Remove the dough from the bowl and place it on a lightly floured work surface.

Divide the dough into 3 equal pieces and roll them into strips about 8 inches long. Press the 3 strips together at one end and then braid the dough strips, crossing the strip on the left under the middle strip, then the right strip under the middle, and so on 6 or 7 times, until you complete the braid. Pinch the ends together and transfer to the prepared baking sheet. Let rise for another 10 minutes. Whisk the remaining egg in a cup or a bowl and brush the loaf with the egg wash; sprinkle with poppy seeds, if desired. Bake for 25 to 30 minutes, or until golden brown.

CHEF'S NOTE: Feel free to add a little more sugar if you like a sweeter challah.

YIELD: 1 LARGE LOAF

SIMPLICITY: + +

IRISH BROWN SODA BREAD

I was introduced to this particular recipe at a little bed-and-breakfast establishment in Kenmare, "the jewel in the ring of Kerry," in southwest Ireland. It was a cold and rainy morning, and I awoke to the aroma of this bread baking. This vivid moment remains one of my treasured food memories. The bread tasted even better than it smelled, and I asked the B and B owner, Dr. Boland, for the recipe. I've used it often ever since, and here it is. It also makes great toast, and it's perfect for dunking into soups.

4 cups whole-wheat flour

⅓ cup sugar

2 teaspoons baking soda

1 teaspoon kosher salt

6 tablespoons (¾ stick) unsalted butter, diced, plus additional for the baking sheet

2 large eggs

1½ cups buttermilk

Preheat the oven to 400°F.

Lightly butter an 11 by 17-inch baking sheet. In a large bowl, stir together the flour, sugar, baking soda, and salt. Work in the butter with a pastry cutter until the mix resembles course crumbs. Break the eggs into a measuring cup and whisk with a fork. Add the buttermilk to the eggs; there should be 2 cups of liquid (add a little more or less buttermilk as necessary). Pour this mixture into the flour mixture and stir until completely incorporated. Turn out the dough onto a lightly floured work surface, sprinkle with a little flour, and knead with your hands for 3 minutes.

Divide the dough into 3 equal parts and form each into a ball. Using a small, sharp knife, cut an *X* across the top of each ball and transfer the balls to the prepared baking sheet. Bake for 30 minutes, or until a toothpick inserted in the center comes out clean.

CHEF'S NOTES: If you prefer the more traditional white Irish soda bread to brown, simply substitute white flour for the whole-wheat flour. Be sure you don't use self-rising flour, which contains baking powder.

YIELD: 3 SMALL LOAVES

SIMPLICITY: + +

ALA MOANA BANANA BREAD

I think some people will enjoy this recipe so much they will watch their bananas ripen just so they can make it. We have named this distinctly home–style bread after our store in Honolulu, located at the Ala Moana Shopping Center on the edge of Waikiki. It was there we began the tradition of making a sandwich out of this bread with a cream cheese filling. We cut the sandwich in half and use it to garnish our famous Orange Soufflé Salad (you will find a recipe for this salad in our Neiman Marcus Cookbook*)—a presentation we offer now in most of our restaurants across the country.*

2 cups all-purpose flour

¼ teaspoon baking powder

¼ teaspoon baking soda

⅛ teaspoon ground cinnamon

½ cup (1 stick) unsalted butter, plus additional for the loaf pan

¾ cup light brown sugar

2½ cups sliced ripe bananas (about 3 large bananas)

2 tablespoons sour cream

Dash of vanilla extract

2 large eggs

Preheat the oven to 350°F. Generously butter a 9 by 5 by 3-inch loaf pan and set aside.

In a large bowl, sift together the flour, baking powder, baking soda, and cinnamon and set aside. In the bowl of an electric mixer fitted with a paddle attachment, cream the butter and the sugar together on low speed. Add the bananas, sour cream, and vanilla. Mix for 1 minute and then gradually add the flour mixture. When thoroughly incorporated, add the eggs, 1 at a time. Mix well. Pour the batter into the prepared loaf pan and bake for about 1 hour, or until a toothpick inserted in the center comes out clean. Remove from the oven and set the loaf pan on a rack. Let the bread rest in the pan for 10 to 15 minutes before turning out onto the rack to cool.

CHEF'S NOTE: You can pour the batter into muffin tins if you prefer banana muffins to a loaf of banana bread. Bake for 35 to 40 minutes in a 350°F oven.

YIELD: 1 LOAF

SIMPLICITY: +

CHRISTMAS FRUIT BREAD

When Helen Corbitt made these loaves during her heyday in the 1960s, they were wildly popular, so I thought it was only fitting to share the recipe. She baked hundreds during the holiday season and sent them to her friends and Neiman Marcus customers, who no doubt appreciated the gesture. This bread is a little dense, like the traditional German Christmas stollen, and is perfect served warm for afternoon tea or coffee. Do note that this recipe will take the better part of a day from start to finish, but it is well worth the effort.

FOR THE BREAD

½ cup shredded dried citron

½ cup raisins, chopped

½ cup dried or candied cherries, chopped

1 tablespoon grated lemon zest

½ cup chopped blanched almonds

1 teaspoon ground cinnamon

½ teaspoon ground cloves

½ teaspoon grated nutmeg

¼ cup brandy or Amaretto Disaronno

2 tablespoons lukewarm water (about 110°F)

1 package active dry yeast

1 cup milk

8 tablespoons (1 stick) unsalted butter, plus
   additional for the loaf pans

¼ cup sugar

1 teaspoon kosher salt

1 large egg, beaten

4 cups all-purpose flour

FOR THE ICING

½ cup confectioners' sugar

¼ cup milk

Dash of almond extract

Place the citron, raisins, cherries, and lemon zest in a mixing bowl. Add the almonds, cinnamon, cloves, nutmeg, and brandy. Stir well so the ingredients are thoroughly mixed, cover the bowl with plastic wrap, and let sit overnight.

Pour the lukewarm water into the bowl of an electric mixer fitted with a dough hook. Sprinkle the yeast over the water, mix for 30 seconds, and let sit for 5 minutes to soften. Meanwhile, pour the milk into a small saucepan and set over medium-low heat. Bring to a simmer, remove from the heat, and add 5 tablespoons of the butter, the sugar, and the salt. Stir together so the butter melts and then let cool to lukewarm. Transfer the milk mixture to the bowl of the electric mixer and add the beaten egg and 2 cups of the flour. Mix well on low speed and then slowly add the remaining 2 cups flour and mix until incorporated. Remove the bowl from the mixer, cover the dough with a slightly damp towel, and let rise in a warm place until doubled in volume, about 2 hours.

Generously butter 2 loaf pans measuring 9 by 5 by 3 inches and set aside. Turn out the dough onto a lightly floured work surface, sprinkle with a little flour, and knead for 3 or 4 minutes, until the dough becomes firm. Return to a clean bowl, cover with a slightly damp towel, and let rise again until doubled in volume (about 2 hours). Turn out onto a lightly floured work surface and knead the reserved fruit into the dough. Divide the dough evenly in half and place in the prepared loaf pans. Cover the pans with slightly damp towels and let the dough rise until doubled in volume again, about 2 hours.

Preheat the oven to 350°F.

Melt the remaining 3 tablespoons butter and brush the tops of the loaves with it. Transfer the loaves to the oven and bake for 35 to 40 minutes, or until a toothpick inserted in the center comes out clean. Remove from the oven and let the loaves rest in the pans for 15 minutes before turning out onto a rack to cool.

When the loaves are cool to the touch,

they are ready to ice. Place the sugar, milk, and almond extract in a small bowl and mix together with a spoon until smooth. Use a small palette knife or an offset spatula to spread the icing on top of the loaves.

CHEF'S NOTES: Dried citron (the aromatic candied peel) is widely available in specialty stores and many supermarkets during the holiday season. Note that it is best to let the dried fruit marinate in the brandy overnight.

YIELD: 2 LOAVES

SIMPLICITY: ✚ ✚ ✚ ✚

ANITA'S BLUEBERRY-SOUR CREAM
MORNING MUFFINS

This is one of those good old-fashioned sweet morning treats that makes you want to forget your diet. As my English-born coauthor likes to say, this delicacy is "quite more-ish." The recipe was developed by Anita Hirsch, my trusty colleague and Neiman Marcus's corporate chef, who tested many of the recipes in this book and prepared dishes for the book's photographs. We have worked together, off and on, for the last twenty years, ever since we met in the kitchen of the Netherland Plaza Hotel in Cincinnati, and there are days I really don't know what I would do without her.

FOR THE MUFFINS

2½ cups cake flour (not high-gluten)

2 teaspoons baking powder

1 teaspoon baking soda

¼ teaspoon kosher salt

2 large eggs plus 1 large egg yolk

¾ cup (1½ sticks) unsalted butter, melted, plus
   additional for the coffee mugs

1 teaspoon vanilla extract

1 cup sour cream

½ cup buttermilk

1½ cups plus 2 tablespoons sugar

½ pint fresh blueberries, or 1 cup frozen

FOR THE STREUSEL CRUMB TOPPING

1½ cups all-purpose flour

½ cup light brown sugar

2 teaspoons granulated sugar

2 teaspoons ground cinnamon

¼ teaspoon kosher salt

12 tablespoons unsalted butter, cut into small
   pieces

FOR THE GLAZE

½ cup confectioners' sugar

2½ tablespoons heavy cream, half-and-half,
   or milk

Preheat the oven to 350°F. Lightly butter 8 to 10 glazed coffee mugs (see Chef's Note). Place a paper baking cup inside each mug.

To prepare the muffins, sift together the flour, baking powder, baking soda, and salt into a bowl and set aside. In the bowl of an electric mixer fitted with a paddle attachment, mix together the eggs and yolk, melted butter, vanilla, sour cream, and buttermilk. When incorporated, add the sugar and mix for 1 minute longer. Gradually add the flour mixture and mix for about 1½ minutes; it is fine if the batter still has a few lumps. Gently fold in the blueberries with a rubber spatula.

To prepare the streusel topping, place the flour, brown sugar, granulated sugar, cinnamon, salt, and butter in a bowl. Using your fingers, break up the butter and incorporate into the mixture until it becomes coarse and crumbly.

Evenly divide the batter among the prepared coffee mugs and top evenly with the streusel mixture. Place the mugs on a baking sheet and transfer to the oven. Bake for 30 minutes, or until a toothpick inserted in the center comes out clean. Remove from the oven and let the muffins rest for 10 minutes before removing the paper baking cups from the coffee mugs.

To prepare the glaze, mix the sugar and cream in a bowl. Using a fork, drizzle the glaze over the top of the muffins.

CHEF'S NOTE: Using glazed coffee mugs (which have been fired at a high temperature) is important, as unglazed ones are likely to crack in the oven. The coffee mugs give the muffins a straight-sided appearance that invites double-takes. Alternatively, you can bake the muffins in a regular muffin tin.

YIELD: 8 TO 10 MUFFINS

SIMPLICITY: + +

SWEET CINNAMON ROLLS

I love taking our classic Monkey Bread recipe and making it even better. In this recipe, we fold in the cinnamon sugar and then add a creamy frosting to finish it up. Growing up, I knew these as sticky buns; today I know them as sinful! Diet food they're not, but hey, make them for a special occasion.

FOR THE MONKEY BREAD DOUGH

1 cup milk

1 tablespoon plus 1 teaspoon active dry yeast
(1½ packages)

¼ cup sugar

1 teaspoon kosher salt

½ cup (1 stick) unsalted butter, melted, plus
additional for the cake pan

3¼ cups all-purpose flour, sifted

FOR THE SWEET CINNAMON FILLING

½ cup (1 stick) slightly softened unsalted butter

1¼ cups light brown sugar

2 tablespoons granulated sugar

2½ tablespoons ground cinnamon

FOR THE FROSTING

2 ounces cream cheese

1 cup confectioners' sugar

2 tablespoons milk

To prepare the dough, pour the milk into a saucepan and set over medium heat for 2 to 3 minutes, or until lukewarm (but not hot), about 110°F. Transfer the milk to the bowl of an electric mixer fitted with a paddle attachment. (Alternatively, the dough can be mixed by hand in a large bowl.) Add the yeast and a pinch of the sugar and let stand for about 5 minutes, until the yeast is dissolved. Add the remaining sugar, the salt, and the melted butter and gradually stir in the flour for 2 to 3 minutes on low speed, until a soft dough forms. Transfer the dough to a lightly oiled bowl, cover with plastic wrap, and let rise in a warm place for about 1 hour, or until doubled in volume.

While the dough is rising, prepare the cinnamon filling. Place the butter, brown and granulated sugars, and cinnamon in a small bowl and stir until smooth. Set aside.

To prepare the frosting, place the cream cheese in the bowl of an electric mixer fitted with a paddle attachment and beat on low speed for 3 or 4 minutes until soft. (Alternatively, stir by hand.) Add the sugar and milk and mix until incorporated. Set aside.

Preheat the oven to 350°F. Lightly butter a 9 by 11-inch cake pan and set aside.

Turn out the dough onto a lightly floured work surface and roll out to a thickness of ¼ inch (the dough will be about 18 by 14 inches). Spread the cinnamon filling evenly over the dough and then roll up the shorter side of the dough to form a long log. Cut the dough into 12 strips about 1½ inches wide. Lay each slice on the prepared cake pan with the cut side up; it is fine if the rolls are touching one another. Use a second pan if necessary. Let the cinnamon rolls rise in a warm place for 20 minutes.

Bake the rolls for 15 minutes, or until golden brown. Remove the pan from the oven, spread the frosting evenly over all the cinnamon rolls, and serve immediately.

CHEF'S NOTE: Adding raisins and pecans to the filling makes these buns an even better treat.

YIELD: ABOUT 12 ROLLS

SIMPLICITY: + + +

soups

VERY TOMATOEY MINESTRONE

GRILLED VEGETABLE SOUP
with Smoked Cheddar

NEW ENGLAND FISH CHOWDER

COUNTY MAYO PEA SOUP

CHEESE AND ALE SOUP

CHICKEN VELVET SOUP

POTATO AND BACON SOUP

CARAMELIZED ONION SOUP

HYDE PARK SHRIMP BISQUE

GRANDMOM'S TURKEY SOUP

I ALWAYS SAY there are good cooks, and then there are good cooks who can make soup. Over the years, I have come to realize that not every cook can make a good pot of soup; it is an art that takes more than the ability to follow a recipe. For example, soup requires the cook to have a sense of timing that allows the veggies or the meats to brown just enough to begin the right flavor profile, and it requires just the right amount of early seasoning so that when the soup is finished, the flavors have exactly the right balance.

The other thing to remember is that soup is not really finished when the recipe says it is. Sometimes, it's not done for hours or even a day later, when it has had the chance to set up and all the flavors have had time to marry. You've probably told yourself, "I think the soup is better today than it was yesterday"; this illustrates very well how flavor profiling occurs when a pot of soup has a chance to really come together. I am always encouraging our chefs to start making the soup that will be served tomorrow today—so many times, it just plain tastes better! Young chefs sometimes insist that soup must be made fresh, but they are often wrong. Good soup takes time—and I don't mean fresh thyme (although I do love fresh thyme in many of my soups!).

In our restaurants, we go through vast amounts of soup every day. In some restaurants, we serve a *soupe du jour,* which recalls French culinary tradition and classic café–style menus that change every day. In other Neiman Marcus restaurants, we simply refer to it as *today's soup.* In either case, we expect to go through many gallons each day, even in summertime, demonstrating our customers' love of soup. In addition, at most stores, we offer a seasonal soup that remains on the menu for several months; two of these are the Grilled Vegetable Soup (page 50), made with the bounty of fall vegetables, and the County Mayo Pea Soup (page 52), which we like to make with the freshest peas of early spring. It is hard to imagine the holiday season without Grandmom's Turkey Soup (page 62).

I believe the main reason people choose soup when dining out is that they don't want to take the time and effort to make soup at home. Yes, soups take time to prepare, and sometimes they need to simmer for a while on the stove, but I hope that after reading these recipes you become inspired and feel the urge to get into the kitchen and fill your home with the wonderful, satisfying aromas that come from a great pot of yummy ingredients! One last suggestion: Do yourself a favor, now that you have decided to venture into regular soup production, and find a good-quality heavy-bottomed 4- or 5-quart soup pot or saucepan with a matching lid. This pot will reward you for many years to come, and it won't feel as though you are cooking for the multitudes. Remember, there's no such thing as leftover soup—uneaten soup is a meal for tomorrow or even the next day, because like many of us, a good soup just gets better with time.

NOTE ON BLENDING HOT SOUPS

Take care when blending hot soup. Do not overfill the blender, as the hot liquid will expand during mixing and may splatter dangerously; it is best to blend soup in batches. Always put the lid on the blender and use a kitchen towel or an oven mitt to hold the lid in place with one hand. Use the other hand to pulse the blender before turning it on continuously to purée the soup.

VERY TOMATOEY MINESTRONE

Now this is a meal! It's almost a vegetable stew with pasta, beans, and tomatoes, so the consistency is thicker than that of a typical minestrone. Having said that, authentic Italian minestrone has as many variations as there are cooks, as it contains whatever vegetables are in season, favorite beans and pasta (or rice), and, sometimes, meat. Minestrone goes back into the mists of time, when it formed a cornerstone of the Italian peasants' diet and was made every day. It can even be traced to ancient Roman times. Likewise, it has been featured on the Neiman Marcus menu over the years and has become a family favorite. Kids love pasta, and this is a good way to feed them vegetables.

1 cup dried ditalini or small elbow pasta

4 tablespoons olive oil

1 small carrot, peeled, halved, and thinly sliced into half-moons

2 celery stalks, finely diced

1 small onion, thinly sliced

2 garlic cloves, crushed

1 zucchini (unpeeled), halved and thinly sliced into half-moons

1 yellow squash (unpeeled), halved and thinly sliced into half-moons

Salt and freshly ground black pepper to taste

1 can (14 ounces) crushed tomatoes

1 can (14 ounces) tomato purée

2 cups vegetable juice, such as V-8

1 cup Chicken Broth (page 267) or store-bought chicken stock

1 can (14 ounces) cannelini beans (or canned white beans), drained and rinsed

1 cup roughly torn spinach leaves

1 bunch fresh parsley, leaves only, chopped

6 basil leaves, gently torn

¼ cup freshly grated Parmesan cheese

Bring a saucepan of salted water to a boil and add the pasta. Cook according to the directions on the package (typically, 8 to 10 minutes), until just al dente. Drain and set aside. Heat 3 tablespoons of the olive oil in a saucepan over medium heat. When hot, add the carrot, celery, onion, and garlic and sauté for 4 minutes; do not let brown. Add the zucchini and yellow squash, season with salt and pepper, and sauté for 2 minutes longer. Add the tomatoes, tomato purée, vegetable juice, and broth, and bring to a boil. Reduce the heat to medium-low and simmer for 15 minutes. Add the beans and cook for 5 minutes longer. Add the drained pasta and the spinach, parsley, and basil and season again with salt and pepper. Cook the soup for 5 minutes longer. Ladle the soup into serving bowls and top with the Parmesan cheese. Drizzle the remaining 1 tablespoon olive oil over the bowls. Serve with Savory Pretzel Sticks (page 31), Savory Parmesan Popovers (page 27), or your favorite crusty bread.

CHEF'S NOTES: Ditalini is a miniature tube pasta that is typical of the Campagna region, where it features in the classic regional dish of *pasta e fagioli* (pasta and bean soup). The word *ditalini* means "little thimbles" in Italian. If you want to keep this soup vegetarian, substitute Vegetable Broth (page 266) for the chicken broth.

SERVES: 8 (ABOUT 3½ QUARTS)

SIMPLICITY: ✦ ✦ ✦

GRILLED VEGETABLE SOUP
with Smoked Cheddar

I began cooking vegetables on a wood-burning grill during my stint at the Cincinnatian Hotel in the mid-1980s. I really appreciated the new dimension of flavor that grilling gave vegetables, and when we folded them into a stock base and added smoky Cheddar (a wonderful ingredient I have always enjoyed), we found we had a hit on our hands. This makes a great year-round soup now that most people think of grilling as a year-round option. Even at chillier times of the year, consider firing up your propane grill because not only will this soup warm you right up but also you will find it's pleasingly evocative of the warmer months.

1 large carrot, peeled and cut in half lengthwise

1 large zucchini, cut in half lengthwise

1 large yellow squash, cut in half lengthwise

1 poblano chile, cut in half lengthwise, seeds and ribs removed

1 red bell pepper, cut in half lengthwise, seeds and ribs removed

1 large red onion, cut in half crosswise

2 tomatoes, cut in half

1 portobello mushroom, cleaned

4 tablespoons olive oil

3 garlic cloves, minced

1 large shallot, minced

1 cup vegetable juice, such as V-8

1 cup canned crushed tomatoes

3 cups Chicken Broth (page 267) or store-bought chicken stock

1 tablespoon chopped fresh basil

Salt and freshly ground white pepper to taste

8 ounces smoked Cheddar cheese, grated

Prepare the grill. Place the carrot, zucchini, yellow squash, poblano, bell pepper, onion, tomatoes, and mushroom in a large bowl. Add 3 tablespoons of the olive oil and toss all the ingredients together. Arrange the vegetables on the grill and cook over medium-high heat, turning as needed, so the vegetables get attractive grill marks and just start to soften, 3 or 4 minutes on each side; the carrot will take 2 or 3 minutes longer. Remove the vegetables from the grill and set aside to cool. Place the poblano and bell pepper in a kitchen towel and rub the towel vigorously to remove the charred skin; alternatively, use the tip of a sharp knife to peel off the skin. It is fine if a little skin remains. When all the vegetables are cool enough to handle, finely dice them.

Pour the remaining 1 tablespoon olive oil into a large saucepan and set over medium-high heat. Add the diced vegetables, garlic, and shallot and sauté for 5 minutes. Add the vegetable juice, crushed tomatoes, broth, and basil.

Bring the soup to a boil, reduce the heat to low, and simmer for 15 minutes; season with salt and pepper.

Ladle the soup into small crocks and sprinkle the smoked Cheddar over the top just before serving.

CHEF'S NOTES: It helps to have a grill screen or basket for grilling vegetables so you don't lose anything through the grate. Other smoked cheese would work in this recipe, but I prefer Cheddar here because its soft texture makes it a good melting cheese.

SERVES: 6

SIMPLICITY: + + +

NEW ENGLAND FISH CHOWDER

There are many kinds of chowder, and while most people associate them with seafood, that is not a prerequisite. They originated in New England, and the name "chowder" is probably derived from the French-Canadian word chaudière, *"cooking pot." A really good chowder should seem like a simple dish, not too crowded with multiple ingredients or flavors. In this recipe, the fish and potatoes take center stage, which is as it should be. Despite the appearance of simplicity, chowders can be relatively complex to make, involving several steps, but the results are worth the effort when it's done right.*

2 tablespoons olive oil

2 onions, finely diced (peels reserved)

1 large shallot, minced (peels reserved)

2 cloves garlic (peels reserved)

4 sprigs fresh thyme

1 celery stalk, finely sliced

2 pounds fish scraps (see Chef's Notes)

1 cup dry white wine

6 cups half-and-half

6 tablespoons (¾ stick) unsalted butter

1 large Idaho potato (about 1 pound), peeled and
    finely diced

1 pound grouper, Dover sole, or snapper fillets,
    roughly chopped

¼ cup all-purpose flour

1 bunch fresh parsley

Salt and freshly ground white pepper to taste

Heat the olive oil in a large saucepan over medium heat. Add the onion and shallot peels, and then add the garlic, thyme and celery. Sauté for 3 minutes, add the fish scraps, and continue to sauté for 2 minutes longer. Add the white wine and bring to a boil. Reduce the heat to low and simmer for 2 minutes. Add the half-and-half and continue to simmer the fish broth for 30 minutes. Remove the pan from the heat and strain the broth through a fine mesh strainer into a clean saucepan; discard the vegetables and fish scraps.

In a clean saucepan, melt 2 tablespoons of the butter over medium-high heat. Add the onions and shallot, and sauté for 1 minute. Add the potato and the fish and continue to sauté for 2 minutes longer. Add the strained fish broth to the pan, bring to a simmer, and cook for 30 minutes.

Melt the remaining 4 tablespoons butter in a small saucepan over medium heat. Reduce the heat to low and slowly add the flour, stirring continuously with a wooden spoon to form a roux. Cook for 2 minutes and remove from the heat. Whisk the roux mixture into the soup with a wire whisk (add a little less if the soup has already thickened sufficiently). Cook the soup for 8 minutes longer, then add the parsley, and season with salt and pepper. Ladle the chowder into serving bowls.

CHEF'S NOTES: The adventurous home cook might consider buying 4 pounds of whole snapper, 1½ pounds of grouper fillet (skin on), or 2 whole Dover sole fillets, which would yield both enough fish fillets and trimming for the recipe, rather than buying fish scraps separately, as called for in this recipe. If you do buy your fish this way, thoroughly clean it, reserving all the bones and the skin. If buying fish scraps, use the same types of fish, if you have a choice.

SERVES: 6 TO 8

SIMPLICITY: + + + +

COUNTY MAYO PEA SOUP

If you like pea soup, you **love** *it and will probably go anywhere for a good version. So you should know there is a little pub in the picturesque seaside village of Killala on Ireland's west coast where, several years ago, I enjoyed the best pea soup I ever tasted, served in a crusty hollowed-out loaf. As I ate the bread from the inside of the loaf with rich and creamy butter and reflected on the unforgettable, vibrant flavor of the soup, I told myself that here was something worth emulating once I got home. The Irish Brown Soda Bread on page 36 makes a great companion to this soup.*

4 tablespoons (½ stick) unsalted butter

1 onion, finely diced

1 leek, white part only, finely diced

1 small Idaho potato (about 8 ounces),
   peeled and finely chopped

4 sprigs fresh thyme

4 cups Vegetable Broth (page 266) or
   store-bought vegetable stock

2 pounds frozen peas

½ cup heavy cream

Juice of ½ lemon

Salt and freshly ground white pepper to taste

Crispy Croutons (page 279)

Melt 2 tablespoons of the butter in a saucepan over medium heat. Add the onion, leek, and potato and sauté for 3 minutes; do not let brown. Add the thyme and 3 cups of the broth, bring to a boil, and simmer for 10 minutes. Add the peas and continue cooking for 7 minutes longer. Remove the pan from the heat and remove the thyme stems. Transfer the soup to a blender and, with the machine running, add the remaining 1 cup broth (see the note on blending soup on page 47). Return the soup to a clean saucepan and set over medium heat. Add the cream, lemon juice, salt, and pepper. Stir well and warm through. Ladle into serving bowls and top with the crispy croutons.

CHEF'S NOTES: Making this recipe with shelled fresh garden peas (especially spring peas) makes an even more flavorful soup than one using frozen peas. For a more refined version, strain the soup after blending for a silkier consistency.

SERVES: 4 (ABOUT 1¾ QUARTS)

SIMPLICITY: + +

CHEESE AND ALE SOUP

The combination of cheese and beer in soup may be tried and true, but it never floated my boat until one cold winter's day in Stowe, Vermont, where I was working at a resort. After sampling a great version there, everything clicked into place, and the more I have come to appreciate the flavor of good ale over the years, the more this recipe has grown on me. It is important to select a premium beer so that the subtle sweetness acts in balance with the sharpness of a good-quality cheese.

4 tablespoons (½ stick) unsalted butter

1 large onion, finely diced

2 garlic cloves, crushed

4 cups half-and-half

1 pound sharp yellow Cheddar cheese, grated

1 pound Gruyère cheese, grated

2 cups dark ale, such as Bass Ale

1 cup heavy cream

Salt and freshly ground white pepper to taste

Dash of Tabasco sauce

Dash of Worcestershire sauce

Crispy Croutons (page 279)

Melt 2 tablespoons of the butter in a large saucepan over medium-high heat. Add the onion and garlic and sauté for 3 minutes. Add the half-and-half and bring to a boil. Reduce the heat to medium-low and simmer for 5 minutes. Add both cheeses and whisk them in, using a wire whisk, until melted thoroughly, 2 or 3 minutes. Remove the pan from the heat, transfer the soup to a blender in batches (see the note on blending soup on page 47), and blend to a creamy consistency. Return the soup to a clean saucepan and set over low heat. Gradually stir in the ale and cream and bring to a simmer. Season the soup with salt, pepper, Tabasco, and Worcestershire sauce. Ladle the soup into serving bowls and garnish with the crispy croutons.

CHEF'S NOTE: If you own a handheld mixer, you can use it to purée the soup instead of transferring the soup to a blender.

SERVES: 6 TO 8

SIMPLICITY: + +

CHICKEN VELVET SOUP

Reading through Helen Corbitt's recipes from forty and fifty years ago, it's exciting to realize she was ahead of the paradigm shift that has occurred in American food. She paid considerable attention to texture and enjoyed creating layers of flavor, a goal sought by many of today's leading chefs. The velvety smoothness of this soup is a quality she also sought in her chocolate cake (page 218). When you taste this rich and creamy but simple-looking soup for the first time, you'll find it surprisingly light and refreshing.

¼ cup olive oil

1 frying chicken, about 3 pounds, cut into pieces

1 large onion, finely chopped

1 large carrot, finely chopped

1 celery stalk, finely chopped

2 garlic cloves

½ cup dry white wine

3 chicken bouillon cubes, crumbled

3 sprigs fresh thyme

1 bunch fresh parsley (6 to 8 small sprigs reserved
    for garnish)

2 dried bay leaves

8 black peppercorns

1 tablespoon all-purpose flour

6 cups heavy cream

Salt and freshly ground white pepper to taste

Heat the olive oil in a large saucepan over medium heat. Add the chicken pieces and sear them, turning occasionally, 2 or 3 minutes on each side. Remove the chicken pieces and set aside. Add the onion, carrot, celery, and garlic to the same saucepan and sauté for 3 or 4 minutes. Add the wine, bouillon, thyme, parsley, bay leaves, and peppercorns. Add the flour and thoroughly mix together. Return the seared chicken to the pan and mix well. Add the cream and bring the soup to a simmer. Reduce the heat to low and simmer the soup for about 1 hour, or until the chicken meat falls from the bone.

Strain the soup into a clean saucepan, reserving the chicken (discard the vegetables). When it is cool enough to handle, shred the chicken meat (discard the skin and bones) and add it to the soup base. Return the soup to a simmer and adjust the seasoning with salt and pepper. Ladle the soup into serving bowls and garnish with a sprig of fresh parsley.

CHEF'S NOTE: The bouillon cubes add an element of flavor that cannot be replicated with stock or other ingredients. It's a *truc*, or "culinary trick," the great Paul Bocuse taught me.

SERVES: 6 TO 8

SIMPLICITY: + + +

POTATO AND BACON SOUP

Here is a Neiman Marcus recipe that has steadily evolved over the years, and it's hard to imagine it getting any better. The secret to the soup's creamy texture and superb flavor is Yukon Gold potatoes, a variety that has become deservedly popular over the last ten to fifteen years. These potatoes also give the soup a yellow tinge that is warmer than the stark white color of traditional potato soups. The caramelized sugars and smokiness in the maple-cured bacon combine wonderfully with the potatoes.

6 slices maple-cured (or sugar-cured) bacon, diced

6 scallions, finely sliced

1 onion, finely chopped

1 small carrot, peeled and finely chopped

2 garlic cloves

2 pounds Yukon Gold potatoes, peeled and finely chopped

6 cups Chicken Broth (page 267) or store-bought chicken stock

1 cup heavy cream

Salt and freshly ground white pepper to taste

Dash of Worcestershire sauce

6 to 8 fresh parsley sprigs

Heat a large saucepan, add the bacon, and sauté over medium-high heat until crisp and fully cooked. Remove the bacon with a slotted spoon, leaving the fat in the pan, and drain on paper towels. When it is cool, crumble the bacon and set aside. Add the scallions, onion, carrot, and garlic to the same pan and sauté for 5 minutes. Add the potatoes, toss well with the vegetables, and add the broth. Bring to a simmer, reduce the heat to medium, and cook for about 15 minutes, until the potatoes are fork tender. Transfer the ingredients to a blender in batches (see the note on blending soup on page 47). With the machine running, add the cream, and when the soup is completely smooth, season with salt, pepper, and Worcestershire sauce. Return the soup to a clean saucepan and bring to a simmer, stirring occasionally. Ladle the soup into serving bowls and garnish with the reserved crumbled bacon and the parsley sprigs.

SERVES: 6 TO 8

SIMPLICITY: + +

CARAMELIZED ONION SOUP

The key to perfect French onion soup is the process of slowly caramelizing the onions. If you happen to get some burned bits on the bottom of the pan, just cover the pan for a few minutes and turn off the heat. Then scrape off the sticky bits, leaving them in with the onions. Another important step is choosing a good-quality cheese that melts to a crisp—another must when serving this delicious version of the classic onion soup.

4 tablespoons (½ stick) unsalted butter

3 pounds large yellow onions (6 to 8 onions), thinly sliced

1 teaspoon minced garlic

½ tablespoon dried thyme or 8 sprigs fresh wrapped in cheesecloth

1 cup dry sherry

6 cups warm Beef Broth (page 268) or store-bought beef stock

3 cups warm Chicken Broth (page 267) or store-bought chicken stock

2 dried bay leaves

1 tablespoon Worcestershire sauce

Salt and freshly ground black pepper to taste

Garlic Toast (page 280)

12 ounces to 1 pound Gruyère cheese, cut into 12 to 16 slices

Melt the butter in a large saucepan over medium heat. Add the onions, garlic, and dried thyme (if using fresh thyme, add after the liquid is added). Sauté for about 15 minutes, stirring frequently, until the onions are golden brown and caramelized. Add the sherry and deglaze the pan, scraping the bottom of the pan with a wooden spoon to remove all of the solids. Cook for 3 minutes and then add the warm beef and chicken broths. Add the bay leaves and Worcestershire sauce and bring to a boil. Reduce the heat to low and simmer for 25 minutes longer. Adjust the seasoning with salt and pepper and remove the bay leaves.

Preheat the broiler.

Ladle the soup into ovenproof soup bowls. Top each bowl with a garlic toast and 2 slices of Gruyère. Place the bowls on a baking sheet, transfer to the broiler, and cook until the cheese is melted and bubbly, 3 to 5 minutes.

CHEF'S NOTE: I like the balance of flavors that comes from the mixture of the beef and chicken broths. By all means use all of one and none of the other if you prefer.

SERVES: 6 TO 8

SIMPLICITY: + + +

HYDE PARK SHRIMP BISQUE

Back when I learned to make bisques at cooking school, I remember feeling befuddled at how rice was meant to work as a thickening agent. Once I saw for myself how it indeed does the trick, I never looked back, and it turned out to be one of those defining moments in my education as a chef. It was also the first time I cooked with brandy, and I loved the way the flavor worked with shrimp; the two seemed made for each other. This recipe is certainly in the Helen Corbitt tradition: She just loved to cook with brandies, old ports, and Madeira wines.

2 tablespoons olive oil

3 pounds large shrimp, unpeeled

1 onion, finely chopped

1 large carrot, peeled and finely chopped

2 celery stalks, finely chopped

4 garlic cloves

6 sprigs fresh tarragon

¾ cup white rice

½ cup tomato purée

1 cup canned diced tomatoes

6 cups bottled clam broth

½ cup dry white wine

1½ cups heavy cream

½ teaspoon cayenne pepper

Salt and freshly ground white pepper to taste

¼ cup brandy

Heat the olive oil in a large saucepan over medium-high heat. Sauté the shrimp in their shells for 2 minutes and then add the onion, carrot, celery, garlic, and tarragon. Sauté for 3 minutes longer. Add the rice, tomato purée, tomatoes, clam broth, and wine and simmer for 20 minutes, or until the rice is tender. Remove the pan from the heat and transfer the soup to a blender in batches (see the note on blending soup on page 47); purée until smooth. With the back of a ladle, push the mixture through a coarse strainer into a large bowl and then through a fine strainer into a clean saucepan. Bring the soup to a simmer, stir in the cream, and season with cayenne, salt, and pepper. Just before serving, stir in the brandy and then ladle the soup into warm serving bowls.

CHEF'S NOTE: It is important to use a good-quality brandy—at least a VSOP—for best results. If your wallet is on a diet, just buy a small bottle.

SERVES: 6 TO 8

SIMPLICITY: + + + +

GRANDMOM'S TURKEY SOUP

Made just like my grandmom Steph made it, this soup is a terrific way to use up the holiday turkey—and you can use the turkey recipe on page 138 as a starting point. I enjoy the family tradition of making this soup every Thanksgiving evening. It may seem like a chore, but I always reward myself with a hearty bowl before I go to bed. The trick (and the most efficient technique) is to use the same pan the turkey cooked in. No need to clean it, and if you have already made the gravy in it, so much the better! Besides, after you have made this soup, the pan will be a lot easier to scrub. During the holidays, we serve the same version at Neiman Marcus.

1 cooked turkey carcass, broken up as best you can

1 small onion, finely diced

1 celery stalk, finely diced

1 carrot, peeled and finely diced

2 sprigs fresh thyme

1 dried bay leaf

4 black peppercorns

4 quarts Chicken Broth (page 267) or store-bought chicken stock

4 to 6 chicken bouillon cubes, crumbled

1 cup shredded or chopped cooked turkey meat (reserved from the turkey)

Put the turkey carcass, onion, celery, and carrot in the roasting pan the turkey cooked in. Add the thyme, bay leaf, and peppercorns and place on top of the stove, straddling 2 burners. Add the broth to cover about half of the turkey carcass (add water, if necessary). Bring to a boil, turn down the heat, and simmer gently for about 1½ hours; occasionally, using tongs, pull the meat apart from the bones and set aside. As the carcass and ingredients cook down into the pot, remove the bones and skim off the fat with a large spoon. Add the bouillon cubes to taste and then add back the cooked turkey meat. Let cook for 20 minutes longer. Ladle into warm soup bowls and serve.

CHEF'S NOTES: No need to be too fussy about how much meat is left on the carcass—the more the merrier. Be careful before serving this soup to children (adults too), as bones will be lurking unless you diligently handpick and remove them before the end of the cooking process. To make this soup a meal in itself, add your favorite cooked pasta or rice just before serving.

SERVES: 6 TO 8

SIMPLICITY: + +

starters

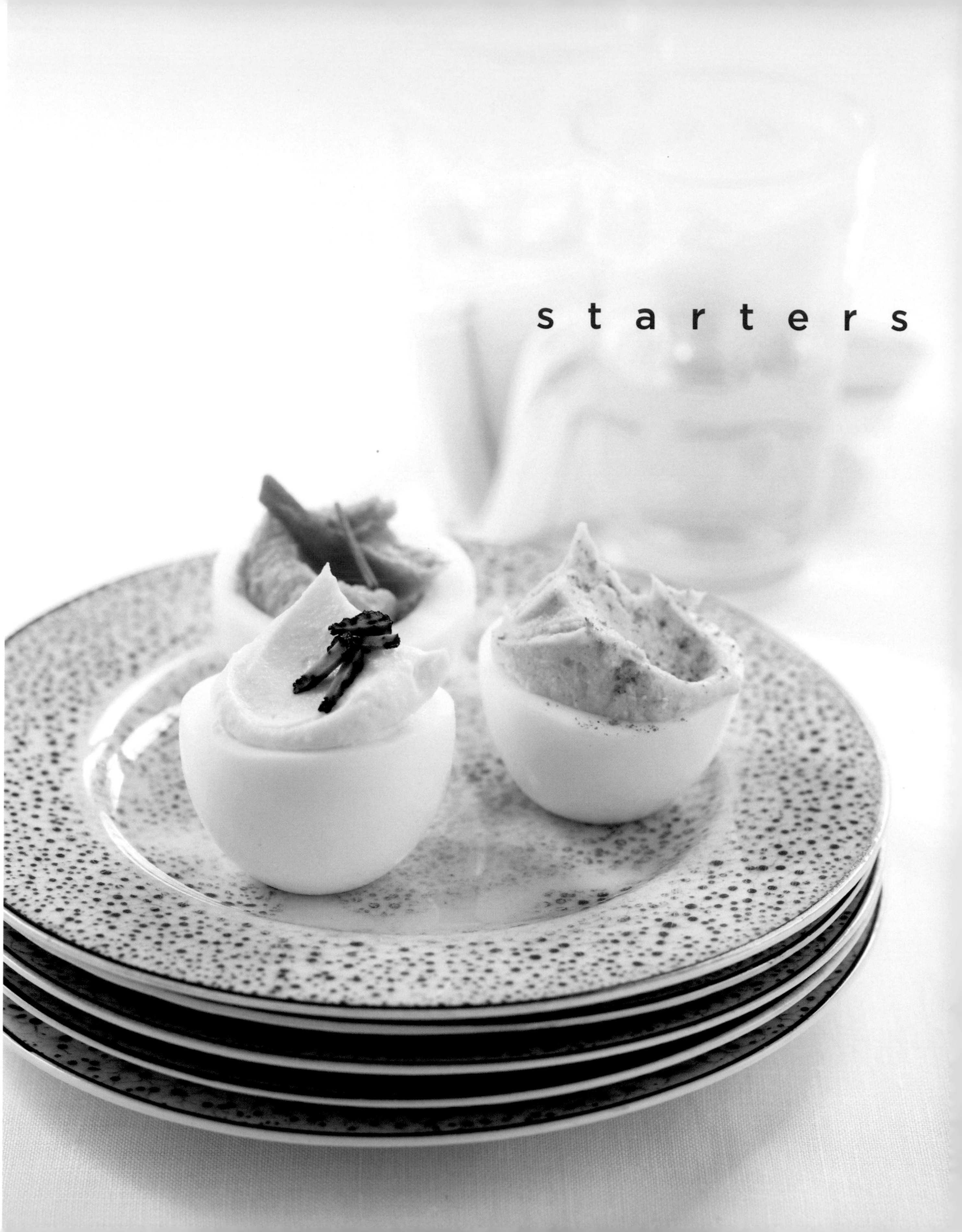

and appetizers

DEVILED EGGS FOUR WAYS

DEVILED PECANS

GOAT CHEESE AND BOURSIN CHEESE LOAF
  with Pear Compote

HUMMUS AND PITA CRISPS

MINI QUICHE LORRAINE

BLUE CHEESE, WALNUT, AND PORT WINE PÂTÉ
  with Melba Toasts

CRABMEAT-GRUYÈRE DIP

LITTLE HAM DELIGHTS

PICKLED SHRIMP

CHILLED MUSSELS GARVINI
  with Gorgonzola Cheese Crostini

BEGGAR'S PURSES

SWISS CHEESE FONDUE
  with Garlic Toast

SHRIMP CORN DOGS

WHITE CHEDDAR CHEESE SOUFFLÉ

GROWING UP in the Garvin household, it seemed we were always getting ready for company. That meant the house got some extra cleaning and all the silver was polished. My mother enjoyed making a great first impression on her guests, and serving appetizers with elegant silverware was an important part of the presentation. I usually jumped on the silver polishing, and I loved to see the gleaming result of all my elbow grease. Today, silver is out of vogue and being used for entertaining less and less, which seems a pity. Around my house, getting ready for company is still about cleaning; we mix and match silverware with a selection of glazed pottery of all different shapes and sizes, and part of the fun is deciding which items we'll use for what foods.

This chapter is all about entertaining, and from what I can gather after reading much material about Helen Corbitt, she was the consummate home entertainer. To this day, people come up to me at the store in Dallas and tell me about times they spent with Helen in her home, and how they were served with great efficiency by Captain White, her lead banquet captain, and his professional staff. I can picture the Little Ham Delights you will find on page 81 or a Mini Quiche Lorraine (page 75) being served butler-style on gleaming silver trays to guests at Helen's home on University Avenue. (As a personal aside, quite coincidentally, my family's house is just two blocks from where Helen resided while she lived and worked in Dallas.)

One of the best features of these recipes is that most of them are designed to be made hours in advance and held either at room temperature or in the refrigerator until your guests arrive. This is important because we always need extra time to get ourselves ready, and those last-minute chores inevitably cause a bit of panic before your company arrives. The last thing you want to be worrying about is putting appetizers together at the last minute.

Today, people are looking for lighter fare and smaller portions. A trend we have seen develop over the years is "grazing"; some of our guests choose two or three appetizers instead of the traditional appetizer and main course or just an entrée. This approach also allows diners to experience more variety and a greater range of flavors. All this has cast more emphasis on appetizers, and as the first impression some guests have of our menu, they are far from an incidental part of the meal—they really make a statement. The same is true at home, where a flavorful, well-textured, and visually appealing appetizer sets the tone for the rest of the meal.

Wherever possible, I like to keep my appetizers seasonal, and when entertaining at home, I always try to choose an appetizer that will set up the main course. Some of the appetizers that follow are more in the style of hors d'oeuvres—mini tastes that are particularly suitable for parties and buffets or as accompaniments to cocktails. What they all have in common is plenty of flavor and plenty of style. Enjoy them!

DEVILED EGGS FOUR WAYS

It's hard to find anyone who doesn't like deviled eggs. Whenever we serve these as a passed hors d'oeuvre, they are always the first item to run out. We also use them to garnish salads. This recipe features four versions: the classic, and variations using smoked salmon, truffle oil, and curry powder. These variations make great talking points, as they dress up a familiar friend like a crisp white shirt worn with an Hermès scarf. Choose your favorite for your next party, or offer them all and win rave reviews! If making deviled eggs ahead of time, cover them with plastic wrap and refrigerate until ready to use.

MY MOTHER'S VERSION (PLAIN)

6 large eggs

3 tablespoons mayonnaise

1 teaspoon dry mustard

½ teaspoon prepared horseradish

Salt and freshly ground white pepper to taste

Pinch of celery salt

Brandy to taste (optional)

1 small piece of red bell pepper, sliced into very
   fine slivers, for garnish

Place the eggs in a large saucepan and cover with water. Bring to a boil and reduce the heat to a simmer; cook the eggs for 7 minutes. Turn off the heat and let the eggs stand in the water for 5 minutes longer. Drain the eggs and let cool. When the eggs are cool enough to handle, peel them and cut in half crosswise. Remove the yolks and place them in a small bowl; crush with the back of a fork. Mash the yolks with the mayonnaise, mustard, horseradish, salt, pepper, and celery salt; add a dash of brandy, if desired. Spoon the yolk mixture back into the egg whites. Transfer to a serving plate and garnish with the red bell pepper slivers.

SERVES: 6

SIMPLICITY: +

SMOKED SALMON DEVILED EGGS

6 large eggs

1 tablespoon cream cheese (about ½ ounce)

2 ounces sliced smoked salmon

1 tablespoon minced fresh dill

½ teaspoon Worcestershire sauce

Salt and freshly ground white pepper to taste

2 black olives, pitted and each cut into 6 strips, for
   garnish

Cook and peel the eggs as in the previous recipe and cut in half crosswise. Remove the yolks and place them in the bowl of a food processor fitted with a metal blade. Add the cream cheese, salmon, dill, Worcestershire sauce, salt, and pepper and blend until smooth. Spoon the yolk mixture back into the egg whites. Transfer to a serving plate and garnish each egg with a piece of black olive.

SERVES: 6

SIMPLICITY: +

TRUFFLE DEVILED EGGS

6 large eggs

3 tablespoons mayonnaise

1 tablespoon truffle oil

½ teaspoon Dijon mustard

Salt and freshly ground white pepper to taste

1 tablespoon minced fresh chives, for garnish

Cook and peel the eggs as in the first recipe and cut in half crosswise. Remove the yolks and place them in the bowl of a food processor fitted with a metal blade. Add the mayonnaise, truffle oil, mustard, salt, and pepper and blend until smooth. Spoon the yolk mixture back into the egg whites. Transfer to a serving plate and garnish with the chives.

SERVES: 6

SIMPLICITY: +

CURRIED DEVILED EGGS

6 large eggs

3 tablespoons mayonnaise

½ tablespoon curry powder

½ teaspoon Dijon mustard

1 teaspoon onion powder

1 teaspoon freshly squeezed lemon juice

Dash of cayenne pepper

Salt and freshly ground white pepper to taste

2 large cherry tomatoes, seeded and julienned, for
  garnish

Cook and peel the eggs as in the first recipe and cut in half crosswise. Remove the yolks and place them in the bowl of a food processor fitted with a metal blade. Add the mayonnaise, curry powder, mustard, onion powder, lemon juice, cayenne, salt, and pepper and blend until smooth. Spoon the yolk mixture back into the egg whites. Transfer to a serving plate and garnish with the tomatoes.

CHEF'S NOTE: If you are feeling especially creative, use a pastry bag fitted with a small star tip to pipe the deviled mixture into the egg whites.

SERVES: 6

SIMPLICITY: +

DEVILED PECANS

Pecans are a Southern crop, one of the foods native to the region, and when Helen Corbitt arrived in Texas from north of the Mason–Dixon, she embraced pecans in her cooking in a big way. We use these spicy nuts as an hors d'oeuvre at all of our bars at Neiman Marcus, and they work well crumbled and sprinkled over salads and even pasta.

1 tablespoon kosher salt

2 teaspoons celery salt

1 teaspoon garlic salt

¼ teaspoon cayenne pepper

2 tablespoons vegetable oil

1 pound shelled pecan halves, or walnuts or
   almonds

Mix the salt, celery salt, garlic salt, and cayenne together in a bowl and set aside. Heat the oil in a heavy-bottomed saucepan over medium heat. When the oil is hot, add the nuts and cook for about 2 minutes, or until they begin to brown; it is important to keep shaking the pan while the nuts are cooking to avoid burning them. Drain the nuts on paper towels. Transfer the nuts to a bowl while still hot and sprinkle with the salt mixture. Mix thoroughly until the nuts are evenly coated. Let cool to room temperature before serving.

CHEF'S NOTE: Consider making a large batch of Deviled Pecans and packaging them attractively for presents during the holiday season.

YIELD: ABOUT 4 CUPS

SIMPLICITY: +

GOAT CHEESE AND BOURSIN CHEESE LOAF
with Pear Compote

Most people love cheese as an appetizer, and here we have reworked a Helen Corbitt cheeseball recipe. Our spin on that classic is to use a combination of goat cheese and herbed Boursin, together with the smoky tones of bacon and toasty caramelized onions. Note that the cheese loaf should be allowed to set up in the refrigerator overnight. The compote can also be made a day ahead; reserve in the refrigerator and bring to room temperature before serving.

FOR THE CHEESE LOAF

6 slices thick-cut maple-cured bacon, diced

1 large onion, thinly sliced

1 tablespoon finely minced fresh thyme

6 ounces fresh goat cheese

1 (5.2 ounce) package Boursin cheese

¼ teaspoon freshly ground black pepper

½ teaspoon kosher salt

FOR THE PEAR COMPOTE

2 tablespoons unsalted butter

1 shallot, finely minced

2 large firm (underripe) pears, peeled, cored, and
    finely diced

2 tablespoons balsamic vinegar

1 tablespoon light brown sugar

Savory Pretzel Sticks with Caraway (page 31)

To prepare the cheese loaf, place the bacon in a skillet and set over medium heat. Cook for 5 or 6 minutes, or until crisp. Remove the bacon and drain on paper towels, leaving the rendered bacon fat in the pan. Add the onion and thyme to the skillet and sauté for about 15 minutes, or until just golden brown. Drain off any excess liquid from the skillet, remove from the heat, and let cool.

Place the goat cheese and Boursin in a food processor and blend until smooth. Add the cooled bacon mixture, blend to incorporate, and season with salt and pepper. Line a 9 by 5-inch loaf pan with plastic wrap and spoon the cheese mixture into the pan. Press the mixture firmly with the back of the spoon and cover with more plastic wrap. Transfer to the refrigerator to chill overnight.

Preheat the oven to 325°F.

To prepare the compote, melt the butter in a small ovenproof skillet over medium-high heat. When the butter begins to foam, add the shallot and pears and cook for 2 minutes. Add the vinegar and sugar, and when the sugar begins to bubble, transfer the skillet to the oven. Bake the compote for 15 minutes. Remove from the oven and let cool.

To serve, turn out the cheese loaf onto a serving platter. Remove the plastic wrap and spoon the cooled pear compote over the cheese loaf. Serve with Savory Pretzel Sticks.

CHEF'S NOTES: Boursin cheese comes in several flavors, and in this recipe we use the type made with garlic and fresh herbs. By all means use ripe fall Granny Smith apples instead of pears in the compote recipe, if you wish.

SERVES: 6 TO 8

SIMPLICITY: + +

HUMMUS AND PITA CRISPS

If you were to drop by my house sometime, chances are you would find homemade hummus in my refrigerator. You would be right in guessing that this simple recipe is a personal favorite—in fact, it is my family's snack and hors d'oeuvre of choice. At Neiman Marcus, we serve this combination on a large platter as a buffet item for private parties.

FOR THE HUMMUS

2 cans chickpeas (15 ounces each), drained

¼ cup plus 1 tablespoon olive oil

1 tablespoon freshly squeezed lemon juice

1 tablespoon ground cumin

1 teaspoon zahtar (see Chef's Note)

¼ cup tahini paste

3 garlic cloves

Salt and freshly ground black pepper to taste

FOR THE PITA CRISPS

3 or 4 pita breads, about 8 inches across

2 tablespoons olive oil

2 garlic cloves, crushed

1 teaspoon kosher salt

To prepare the hummus, place the chickpeas, ¼ cup of the olive oil, the lemon juice, cumin, zahtar, tahini paste, and garlic in a food processor fitted with a metal blade. Season with salt and pepper and blend until smooth. (If the mixture is too thick, add up to ¼ cup more olive oil, 1 tablespoon at a time.) Transfer to a bowl and refrigerate for at least 2 hours to let the flavors marry.

Prepare the grill. (Alternatively, heat a cast-iron skillet.)

Brush the pitas on both sides with the olive oil and then rub with the garlic. Season with the salt and transfer to the grill; set over medium heat. Grill the first side for about 30 seconds and then turn over and toast the other side, being careful not to burn the pitas. Remove the bread and cut into wedges. Keep warm under a cloth until serving.

To serve, place the hummus in a bowl on a serving platter and drizzle with the remaining 1 tablespoon olive oil. Surround the hummus with assorted olives, sliced cucumbers, and the grilled pita bread.

CHEF'S NOTE: Zahtar is a traditional Middle Eastern and North African seasoning blend made from sesame seeds, thyme, and sumac, a tart, dark red tree berry. You can purchase zahtar from a Middle Eastern store or sources online. Use a sprinkling of it as an optional garnish.

SERVES: 6 TO 8

SIMPLICITY: +

MINI QUICHE LORRAINE

Quiche has undeservedly earned a bad rap, what with the "real men don't eat quiche" jibe and the dainty impression some folks have of it. I think of it as a classic with staying power, and it makes a good medium for all kinds of ingredients and flavors. Smoked ham and Gruyère cheese make it comfort food at its best. Helen Corbitt served several quiches at Neiman Marcus, and this is my adaptation of her Lorraine recipe.

FOR THE QUICHE CRUST

1 tablespoon all-purpose flour

1 sheet frozen puff pastry (14 ounces)

FOR THE QUICHE LORRAINE CUSTARD

10 slices thick-cut maple-cured bacon, diced

2 teaspoons olive oil

1 large onion, thinly sliced

6 large eggs

2 cups heavy cream

½ teaspoon dry mustard

Dash of grated nutmeg

Salt and freshly ground white pepper to taste

4 ounces smoked ham, chopped

8 ounces Gruyère cheese, grated

Preheat the oven to 400°F.

To prepare the crust, lightly flour a work surface and roll out the puff pastry with a rolling pin so it fits a rimmed 11 by 17-inch baking sheet with an overlap of ½ inch on each side. Prick the pastry lightly with a fork and cover with another baking sheet the same size. Weight the top sheet with dried beans or pastry weights. Transfer to the oven and bake for about 20 minutes, or until the pastry is a light golden brown. Remove from the oven; set aside the upper pan along with the beans or weights and reserve the baked pastry crust in the pan.

Reduce the oven temperature to 325°F.

To prepare the quiche custard, place the bacon in a skillet and cook over medium heat until crisp, 5 or 6 minutes. Drain the bacon on paper towels and, when it is cool, crumble it. Discard the rendered bacon fat. In the same skillet, heat the olive oil over medium-high heat. Sauté the onion for 5 or 6 minutes, or until lightly browned. Scrape the onions into a bowl and let cool.

In a bowl, beat together the eggs and the cream and season with the mustard, nutmeg, salt, and pepper. Sprinkle the bacon, sautéed onion, ham, and cheese evenly over the pastry crust and pour over the cream and egg custard. Transfer to the oven and bake for 25 to 30 minutes, or until the custard is set. Remove from the oven and cut the quiche into 3½- to 4-inch squares.

CHEF'S NOTE: Most people have heard of quiche Lorraine, named for a region of eastern France, but in fact the dish originated in neighboring Germany.

SERVES: 8 TO 12

SIMPLICITY: + + +

BLUE CHEESE, WALNUT, AND PORT WINE PÂTÉ

with Melba Toasts

Here is a recipe that will delight all blue cheese lovers. Even if you're not a fan of blue cheese, you really should give this pâté a try because Maytag blue's great qualities are its mild flavor and creamy consistency. We tried this recipe with several types of blue cheese, but the domestic Maytag won the taste test. Blue cheese, walnuts, and port are a classic combination, so this delicious appetizer is a natural winner! Note that the pâté and the toasts should be prepared a day ahead.

FOR THE PÂTÉ

4 tablespoons (½ stick) unsalted butter, at room
　temperature

1 pound Maytag or other creamy blue cheese,
　at room temperature

4 tablespoons cream cheese (about 2½ ounces),
　at room temperature

½ cup toasted walnuts (page 281), chopped

⅓ cup port wine

FOR THE MELBA TOASTS

Garlic and Herb Monkey Bread (page 24),
　cut into ⅛-inch-thick slices

Preheat the oven to 350°F.

To prepare the pâté, place the softened butter, blue cheese, and cream cheese in the bowl of an electric mixer fitted with a paddle attachment. Mix on low speed for 20 seconds to lightly fold the ingredients together. Add the toasted walnuts and mix again for 10 seconds to incorporate. Scrape down the sides of the bowl with a rubber spatula.

Pour the port into a small saucepan and set over medium heat. Bring to a simmer and reduce for about 3 minutes, or until it begins to turn syrupy and the bubbles on the surface begin to shine. Remove from the heat and, using a rubber spatula, scrape the hot syrup into the mixer bowl and mix on low speed for 5 seconds.

Line a 2-quart ceramic mold or loaf pan with wax paper, leaving about 5 inches of excess paper over each side. Using a spatula, fold the cheese mixture into the mold and evenly spread the pâté with the spatula. Fold over the wax paper and press it down evenly on the pâté.

Tap the mold lightly on a work surface to be sure any air pockets are released. Refrigerate overnight.

Preheat the oven to 200°F.

To prepare the melba toasts, place the slices of monkey bread on 2 cookie sheets or baking sheets. Transfer to the oven and lightly toast for 4 to 6 hours or, preferably, overnight (in which case, turn off the oven after 4 hours).

To serve the pâté, first unmold it by submerging the bottom half of the mold in a sink or a large bowl filled with hot water for about 30 seconds. Place a serving platter over the mold and invert the mold onto the platter. Use a small spatula to smooth the surface of the pâté and serve with the toasts.

CHEF'S NOTES: I like to garnish the pâté with sliced pears or sliced apples that have been dipped in a little lemon water. If you wish, garnish the platter with small clusters of red, green, and black grapes.

The name *Maytag* probably rings a bell, and sure enough, the family that brought you those reliable appliances established the Iowa dairy the name comes from in 1941. Maytag blue is a semihard, unpasteurized cow cheese that's made by hand and aged twice as long as most blue cheeses.

SERVES: 6 TO 8

SIMPLICITY: + +

A Neiman Marcus menu from the early 1950s.

NEIMAN-MARCUS PENTHOUSE

LUNCHEON TUESDAY, AUGUST 19TH

MENU

STRICTLY PERSONNEL

HERE'S WHAT WE LIKE
ABOUT THE PENTHOUSE..:
THE GOOD FOOD
THE PLEASANT SURROUNDINGS
THE CONVENIENCE

AND...
BECOMING BETTER
ACQUAINTED WITH
OTHERS IN THE STORE

WE HOPE YOU'LL
ALL MAKE IT A
HABIT TO EAT IN
THE PENTHOUSE <u>EVERY</u>
DAY

<u>Memo</u>: Don't forget to give the names of any college girls you know to Dorothy Harris, Younger Set Shop

SOUPS
Cold Beet Borscht with Clotted Cream and Egg Slices
.15

ENTREES
Savory Sweetbreads, Penthouse Style "All Buttoned Up" with Mushrooms, Browned New Potatoes - French Fried Onion Rings
.35

SALADS
Wooden Bowl centered with Artichoke Heart, surrounded with Fresh Garden Greens, Red Ripe Tomato Quarters and Olives - French Dressing
.35

Fruit Plate- A Luscious Melon Ring Filled with Fresh Fruits and Topped with an Ice - Assorted Tea Sandwiches
.35

(Entree and Salad Prices Include a Drink)

SANDWICHES
Ham and Cheese Triangles - centered with Colorful Tomato Aspic Mold - Spiced Pickle Garnish
.20

Cream Cheese and Ripe Olives on Nut Bread - Spiced Seckel Pear
.20

DESSERTS
Lemon Meringue Pie or Caramel Pie
.10

Ice Cream or Ice Cream Sandwiches
.10

Coffee   Tea   Milk
.05

ALL ITEMS ARE CASH - NO TIPPING ALLOWED

CRABMEAT-GRUYÈRE DIP

Back in the 1950s and '60s, when Helen Corbitt was serving her artichoke and cheese dip at Neiman Marcus, you might expect to see it presented at elegant cocktail party buffets alongside chafing dishes and crystal stemware. By adding crabmeat to the recipe, I admit, I have pushed the dip into the realm of decadence, befitting its stylish origins. This recipe gives you a great excuse to bring out those heirloom serving pieces that are used all too rarely!

2 tablespoons unsalted butter, plus additional for the baking dish

1 tablespoon minced shallots

1 cup sliced white mushrooms

1 tablespoon all-purpose flour

2 large egg yolks

1 cup heavy cream

2½ cups grated Gruyère cheese (about 7 ounces)

1 pound jumbo lump crabmeat

Brandy to taste

1 tablespoon Worcestershire sauce

Dash of Tabasco sauce

1 tablespoon chopped fresh parsley

⅛ teaspoon cayenne pepper

Salt and freshly ground white pepper to taste

1 cup cracker crumbs, such as Saltines, crushed with a rolling pin

Preheat the oven to 350°F. Generously butter a 10-inch gratin dish.

Melt the butter in a skillet over medium heat. Add the shallots and mushrooms and sauté for 1 minute. Add the flour to the skillet, stir to form a paste, and then turn off the heat. In a bowl, whisk together the eggs and cream and add the mixture to the skillet. Slowly bring to a simmer over medium-low heat, whisking to break up any lumps. Add the cheese and simmer for 30 seconds, or until it reaches a creamy consistency. Transfer the mixture to a large bowl and stir in the crabmeat, brandy, Worcestershire sauce, Tabasco, parsley, cayenne, salt, and pepper. Pour the crabmeat mixture into the prepared gratin dish and top with the cracker crumbs. Bake for 30 minutes, or until browned on top. Serve with slices of fresh crusty French bread.

CHEF'S NOTE: The flavor and melting texture of Gruyère make it ideal for this recipe. Emmenthal makes an acceptable substitute, but avoid a domestic Swiss, which has neither the same sharpness nor consistency.

SERVES: 8 TO 12

SIMPLICITY: + +

LITTLE HAM DELIGHTS

When I came across this recipe in Helen Corbitt's files, I was unsure what these retro-named morsels would be like to eat. I was delighted to find they were crisp on the outside, light and creamy inside, and as tasty as all get-out. These croquettes are the kind of party food people used to make in the 1950s and '60s, and I guarantee that if you make them once, you will come back to this recipe again and again. The dipping sauce also makes a great spread for sandwiches.

FOR THE GRAINY MUSTARD DIPPING SAUCE

1 cup whole-grain mustard

½ cup Dijon mustard

½ cup mayonnaise

2 tablespoons Worcestershire sauce

FOR THE HAM DELIGHTS

5 large egg whites

8 ounces grated Parmesan cheese

8 ounces ham, ground in a food processor

1 tablespoon all-purpose flour

Salt and freshly ground white pepper to taste

1½ cups vegetable oil

3 large eggs

2 cups dry bread crumbs

To prepare the dipping sauce, place the mustards, mayonnaise, and Worcestershire sauce in a bowl and combine thoroughly. Keep refrigerated.

To prepare the Ham Delights, beat the egg whites in a bowl until stiff peaks form. Add a drop of water to help keep the egg whites stiff. Add the cheese, ham, and flour and season with salt and pepper. Stir gently to avoid overmixing and form into little football shapes.

Preheat the oven to 250°F and heat the oil in a saucepan to 325°F.

Whisk the eggs in a bowl and place the bread crumbs on a plate. Dip each Ham Delight into the beaten eggs and then the bread crumbs. Repeat to create a double coating. Fry 5 or 6 of the croquettes at a time for 4 or 5 minutes, or until lightly brown. Use a slotted spoon to transfer the croquettes to paper towels to drain, then transfer to a cookie sheet and keep warm in the oven until ready to serve. Repeat for the remaining croquettes.

CHEF'S NOTE: Frying only a few of the Ham Delights at a time prevents the temperature of the oil from dropping too much, which would make them soggy rather than crisp.

SERVES: 6 TO 8

SIMPLICITY: + + +

PICKLED SHRIMP

I have often offered pickled shrimp on my menus as an appetizer, dating back to my days as a chef in Cincinnati. Well, great minds think alike, because it turns out Helen Corbitt did likewise at Neiman Marcus. This, then, is a hybrid of our recipes. When you prepare the shrimp, it is important to avoid leaving them in the pickling dressing too long, or they will become rubbery.

FOR THE SHRIMP

1 onion, finely diced

1 carrot, peeled and finely diced

1 jalapeño, halved lengthwise, with seeds

1 lemon, halved

2 teaspoons kosher salt

1 tablespoon pickling spice

1 dried bay leaf

1 pound jumbo shrimp (16 to 20 shrimp), unpeeled

FOR THE PICKLING DRESSING

1 cup cider vinegar

1 large shallot, minced

2 garlic cloves, crushed

1 tablespoon kosher salt

1 teaspoon light brown sugar

Cayenne pepper to taste

2 tablespoons chopped fresh parsley

1 tablespoon chopped fresh tarragon

¼ cup olive oil

To cook the shrimp, pour 6 cups water into a saucepan fitted with a lid and add the onion, carrot, jalapeño, lemon, salt, pickling spice, and bay leaf. Cover, bring to a boil, and then turn down the heat and simmer for 5 minutes. Add the shrimp, and when they start to float to the surface, turn off the heat and let the remaining shrimp rise to the surface. Discard half of the cooking liquid, then add about 3 cups ice to the shrimp liquid and let cool for 1 hour at room temperature.

While the shrimp are cooling, prepare the pickling dressing. In a small saucepan, combine 2 tablespoons water with the vinegar, shallot, garlic, salt, sugar, cayenne, parsley, and tarragon. Bring to a simmer over medium heat, cook for 1 minute, then turn off the heat. Slowly whisk in the olive oil and set aside.

Drain the chilled shrimp, remove the shells and tails, and devein. Transfer the shrimp to a bowl and toss with the pickling dressing. Marinate in the refrigerator for 20 to 30 minutes before serving. For an attractive presentation, fill a large serving bowl with crushed ice. Remove the shrimp from the pickling liquid and arrange on top of the ice. Serve the pickling dressing on the side as a dip.

CHEF'S NOTE: This dish can be prepared ahead. After cooking the shrimp, remove them from the liquid, cover tightly, and chill overnight in the refrigerator.

SERVES: 6

SIMPLICITY: + + +

CHILLED MUSSELS GARVINI
with Gorgonzola Cheese Crostini

When I was working at Cipriani's, an Italian fine-dining restaurant in Steamboat Springs, Colorado, our seafood purveyor once delivered extra mussels by mistake. Using this serendipity to benefit my guests, I created this dish and named it after my Italian alter ego! The dish proved so popular, we had to order those extra mussels on a regular basis. You will have to allow me creative license when it comes to the crostini; the term usually refers to individual slices of toasted bread, but here, the bread is cooked in loaf form and is separated by your hungry guests. I have to warn you that the crostini are lethally addictive, which is why I cook it in quantity, in loaf form. It has become a great favorite at Neiman Marcus.

FOR THE MUSSELS

2 tablespoons unsalted butter

1 large shallot, minced

2 garlic cloves, minced

6 sprigs fresh thyme

6 sprigs fresh tarragon

2 pounds fresh mussels (30 to 35)

1 cup dry white wine

⅓ cup white wine vinegar

½ cup olive oil

Salt and freshly ground white pepper to taste

FOR THE CROSTINI

8 ounces Gorgonzola cheese, at room temperature

2 tablespoons unsalted butter, at room temperature

1 loaf French bread

2 tablespoons grated Parmesan cheese

To prepare the mussels, melt the butter in a large saucepan over medium-high heat. Add the shallot, garlic, 2 sprigs of thyme, and 2 sprigs of tarragon. Stir with a wooden spoon and sauté for 1 minute. Add the mussels and combine with the ingredients in the pan. Add the wine, cover the saucepan, and steam for about 4 minutes, or until the mussel shells have opened; discard any that remain closed. Using a slotted spoon, transfer the mussels to a bowl and set aside. Pour the cooking liquid from the pan into a separate bowl and, using a wire whisk, add the vinegar. Chop the remaining 4 sprigs each of thyme and tarragon and add to the bowl. Slowly whisk in the olive oil in a steady stream and season with salt and pepper. Pour this dressing over the mussels and mix well. Cover tightly with plastic wrap, transfer to the refrigerator, and chill for at least 2 hours before serving.

Preheat the oven to 350°F.

While the mussels chill, prepare the crostini. Place the Gorgonzola cheese and butter in a food processor fitted with a metal blade and blend together. Cutting through only three-quarters of the way, cut the bread into ½-inch slices; be sure not to cut through the loaf. Use a spatula to carefully spread some of the cheese mixture between the bread slices. Push the loaf back together, spread the remaining butter mixture on top, and sprinkle with the Parmesan cheese. Place on a baking sheet, transfer to the oven, and bake for about 20 minutes, or until the loaf begins to brown. Serve hot from the oven.

Arrange the chilled mussels in a large serving bowl and serve with the hot Gorgonzola crostini.

CHEF'S NOTE: Sometimes you will have to clean the mussels if they appear sandy or still have a beard attached to the shell. The best way to clean mussels is to soak them in water and scrub them with a plain wire scrub pad. Pull off the beards with your fingers. Rinse the mussels well under cold running water before cooking.

SERVES: 6 TO 8

SIMPLICITY: + +

BEGGAR'S PURSES

Perhaps we should rename this dish Feta in Filo, as Neiman Marcus is not best known for its selection of inexpensive purses! The name, of course, refers to a modest bag containing all one's worldly possessions, like the hobo image of a tied-up handkerchief on the end of a stick. For chefs, a surprise package inside an attractive pastry crust can make a great presentation. These crispy morsels fly out the door at our catering events, and the creamy interior contrasts perfectly with the crunchy outside.

2 cups drained, rinsed, and crumbled feta cheese

1 cup Velouté Sauce (page 278), cooled to room temperature

1 large egg plus 2 large egg yolks

Dash of cayenne pepper

Dash of grated nutmeg

Salt and freshly ground white pepper to taste

1 package (16 ounces) filo dough, thawed

½ cup (1 stick) unsalted butter, melted

Place the feta cheese in a large bowl and add the velouté, eggs, cayenne, nutmeg, salt, and pepper. Cover the bowl with plastic wrap and chill in the refrigerator for at least 1 hour.

Unfold the filo sheets on a clean work surface and cover with a damp kitchen towel. Work with 1 sheet of filo at a time, removing each from beneath the towel and placing it on a clean work surface. Fold the filo sheet in half and brush the entire top surface with butter. Fold in half again to create a square and brush with butter again. Place 1 heaping teaspoon of the feta mixture onto the center of the filo square and pull the corners of the dough together to form a purse, twisting the ends together to secure. Brush the outside of the purse again with butter and place on a large, unbuttered cookie sheet or baking sheet. Chill in the refrigerator for at least 1 hour.

Preheat the oven to 400°F.

Bake the filo purses for 15 to 20 minutes, or until golden brown. Serve hot.

CHEF'S NOTE: Filo dough, of Greek origin, is sold in the frozen section of supermarkets and specialty stores. If when you open the box the dough appears to be broken, it has probably been sitting around for a while. It's best to buy filo at stores that specialize in upscale food ingredients.

SERVES: 8

SIMPLICITY: + +

SWISS CHEESE FONDUE
with Garlic Toast

Fondues are back. All the rage in the 1950s and '60s but barely tolerated in the '70s as kinda square, fondues were out of fashion for quite a while—until the new century dawned. Then it was as though fondue was rediscovered; it was so retro, it was back in again. The key to good fondue is to keep the cheese mixture warm. If you don't own a fondue set, invite your friends into the kitchen and allow them to gather around the saucepan. At Neiman Marcus, we serve fondue for catering events and banquets, and it makes a great party icebreaker.

Garlic Toast (page 280)

2 tablespoons unsalted butter

2 garlic cloves, minced

2 tablespoons all-purpose flour

1 cup heavy cream

8 ounces Gruyère cheese, grated

¼ cup dry white wine, or more to taste

Salt and freshly ground white pepper to taste

Prepare the garlic toast and set aside.

To prepare the fondue, place the butter in a small saucepan and melt it over medium heat. When the butter has melted, add the garlic and sauté for 30 seconds. Add the flour and stir constantly with a wooden spoon to make a roux. Remove the pan from the heat. Pour the cream into a microwavable bowl and heat in the microwave for 1 minute. Return the roux to a low heat and pour in the hot cream while whisking. Continue to whisk until the mixture is incorporated and creamy. Remove the pan from the stove and add the cheese, whisking well until the cheese melts. When the cheese thickens, pour in the wine and return to the stove over low heat. Keep whisking until the consistency is creamy; season with a dash of salt and pepper.

Set up a fondue pot, pour the cheese mixture into the pot, and keep warm. Serve with the garlic toast.

CHEF'S NOTE: As an alternative to the garlic toast, use Melba Toast (page 76) or Savory Pretzel Sticks with Caraway (page 31).

SERVES: 8

SIMPLICITY: + +

SHRIMP CORN DOGS

These are not your everyday State Fair—type corn dogs; this is seriously gussied-up finger food for the most discriminating palate. We get orders for these all the time, and I think people love deep-fried shrimp because it's such a great comfort food. Most comfort foods involve good memories, and these tasty morsels have a knack of bringing those favorite times back.

FOR THE SHRIMP

1 tablespoon pure chili powder

1 teaspoon kosher salt

1 teaspoon freshly ground black pepper

1 pound large shrimp (about 24), peeled, deveined, and tails removed

FOR THE CORN DOG BATTER

3 large eggs

½ cup buttermilk

1 cup milk

¼ cup (½ stick) unsalted butter, melted

¾ cup all-purpose flour

1 cup yellow cornmeal

1 cup dry pancake mix, such as Bisquick

1 tablespoon sugar

1 tablespoon pure chili powder

1 teaspoon kosher salt

½ teaspoon baking powder

Pinch of cayenne pepper

6 cups vegetable oil, for deep frying

¼ cup all-purpose flour, for dredging

Grainy Mustard Dipping Sauce (page 81)

To prepare the shrimp, place the chili powder, salt, and pepper in a bowl and stir together. Add the shrimp, toss, and keep refrigerated.

To prepare the batter, whisk together the eggs, buttermilk, milk, and butter in a bowl. Pour the flour, cornmeal, and pancake mix into a large bowl; add the sugar, chili powder, salt, baking powder, and cayenne and combine thoroughly. Pour the egg mixture into the dry ingredients and mix until smooth. Let the batter rest for 10 minutes.

Pour the vegetable oil into a deep fryer or a large, heavy saucepan and heat until the temperature reaches 350°F. Meanwhile, thread each shrimp onto a skewer at least 4 inches long, with the tail end facing down. Dip the shrimp into the flour and then into the batter. Carefully lower the shrimp into the hot oil without letting go of the skewer. Wait for 2 seconds and then drop the stick and the shrimp into the oil. Fry only 4 shrimp at a time so the oil does not cool too much. Deep-fry for about 1 minute, or until the shrimp turn golden brown, then remove with a slotted spoon and drain on paper towels. Serve with the mustard dipping sauce.

CHEF'S NOTE: If preparing a double batch (or even more) for a party, preheat the oven to 250°F and keep the cooked shrimp warm on cookie sheets. If you want them crispier when you are ready to serve, quickly refry them for 20 seconds.

SERVES: 6 TO 8 AS AN APPETIZER
(24 SHRIMP CORN DOGS)
SIMPLICITY: + + + +

WHITE CHEDDAR CHEESE SOUFFLÉ

This is another sophisticated appetizer and Corbitt favorite that's light, flavorful, and almost regal in its elegance. The soufflé base makes the recipe dependable—and reheatable, a plus for entertaining. You can bake the soufflé 2 or 3 hours ahead of time, hold at room temperature, and then reheat in the oven, covered with foil, at 325°F for 5 or 6 minutes, or until hot in the middle; it will spring back to life perfectly. If you make the soufflé a day ahead, store it in the refrigerator and then reheat in an oven at the same temperature for 25 to 30 minutes.

3 tablespoons unsalted butter, plus additional for the baking dish

¼ cup all-purpose flour

2 cups milk

1 teaspoon kosher salt

Dash of cayenne pepper

1 teaspoon Dijon mustard

Dash of Worcestershire sauce

2 cups grated white Cheddar cheese

6 large eggs, separated

Preheat the oven to 325°F. Generously butter a 2-quart ovenproof baking dish.

In a saucepan, melt the butter over low heat and stir in the flour using a wooden spoon. Cook for 2 minutes, stirring constantly, and then, using a wire whisk, mix in the milk, salt, cayenne, mustard, and Worcestershire sauce, whisking until smooth. Return to a boil and cook for 1 minute longer, whisking constantly. Remove the pan from the heat and let cool for 3 minutes. Stir in the cheese and set aside.

Place the egg yolks in one bowl and the egg whites in another. Whisk the egg yolks until thick and creamy and then stir them into the cheese mixture. Beat the egg whites until stiff and then gently fold them into the cheese and yolk mixture with a spatula. Pour into the prepared baking dish and place in a water bath (a larger baking pan containing hot water that comes halfway up the sides of the dish containing the soufflé mixture). Transfer to the oven and bake for 2 hours, or until lightly golden and a

toothpick inserted in the center comes out clean.

To serve, remove the baking dish from the oven and spoon the soufflé onto warm serving plates.

CHEF'S NOTES: Other types of cheese that work well in this recipe are Gruyère and Fontina. This appetizer calls out for a glass of champagne or sweet Sauternes.

SERVES: 8 TO 10

SIMPLICITY: + +

s a l a d s

NETHERLAND CHOPPED SALAD
with Green Goddess Dressing

MADISON AVENUE SALAD
with Creamy Roquefort Dressing

HEARTS OF PALM SALAD
with Red French Dressing

NEIMAN MARCUS FRUIT SALAD IN A MELON BASKET
with Poppy Seed Dressing

"SALAD MORE THAN"
with Orange Vinaigrette

SPRING SALAD KILKENNY
with Creamy Herb Vinaigrette

THE HIRSCHES' SUNDAY SALAD
with JG House Vinaigrette

WHENEVER I DISCUSS the position of chef with young people looking to enter the culinary world, I always advise them to attend the best culinary school they can afford. Of course, I also like to mention my partiality to the Culinary Institute of America in Hyde Park, New York, my alma mater. Another suggestion I usually make is that they seek to spend quality time in the cold kitchen (otherwise referred to as the pantry or garde-manger station) of a good restaurant. This is where the salads and cold dressings are prepared. All too often, young cooks think this area is only for those unable to handle hot kitchen stoves, but the truth is that some of the most elaborate and exciting dishes in the restaurant are the fancy, creative salads that emerge from this station.

Early in my career, I had the good fortune to work in the pantry kitchens of two great properties: the Top Notch Inn on the Mountain Road, a four-star resort in

Stowe, Vermont, and the Amfac Hotel in Minneapolis. I learned a huge amount about prepping and elaborately decorating salads and other cold platters, and what I learned stayed with me.

Salads have always played an important role on the menus of Neiman Marcus, especially at lunchtime. For many of our customers, eating well and eating light means salads. All of the salads included in this chapter have been carefully created with a "wow! factor" in mind, so that when they are presented to your guests, they will make a great conversation piece. Of course, they will also please the palate. I've made a point of describing the final presentation, but remember that practice always helps; don't attempt these salads for a special occasion before you have had the chance to try them out on your own family. They will love being guinea pigs and taste-testers!

One final piece of advice: I always recommend mixing and serving salads in wooden bowls because the leaves acquire a more uniform coating of dressing. A seasoned wooden bowl also imparts a better flavor to salads. Be sure to wash the bowl by hand rather than in a dishwasher, which would shorten its life span.

NETHERLAND CHOPPED SALAD
with Green Goddess Dressing

I was introduced to this salad when I was executive chef of the Netherland Plaza Hotel in Cincinnati in the mid–1980s—hence the name. It was the first time I was in charge of a large kitchen, and I wanted to change the chopped iceberg salad I inherited on the menu. I was told it was a sacred cow much loved by the hotel guests, so it stayed, but as I moved on through the years, I adapted and tweaked it. Everywhere I have been the chef, it has always been a bestseller; there is something about the appeal of neatly manicured matchstick-size ingredients that gives this kind of salad a timeless popularity.

FOR THE GREEN GODDESS DRESSING

1 cup sour cream

1 cup mayonnaise

¼ cup roughly chopped fresh parsley

3 tablespoons roughly chopped fresh tarragon leaves

2 tablespoons roughly chopped scallion (green part only)

2 anchovies

¼ teaspoon minced garlic

¼ cup cider vinegar

1 teaspoon Worcestershire sauce

Salt and freshly ground white pepper to taste

FOR THE SALAD

1 large head iceberg lettuce, thinly sliced

⅓ cup julienned cooked smoked ham (⅛-inch strips)

⅓ cup julienned cooked turkey breast (⅛-inch strips)

⅓ cup julienned Swiss cheese (⅛-inch strips)

¼ cup peeled and julienned carrots (⅛-inch strips)

¼ cup julienned zucchini (⅛-inch strips)

¼ cup julienned canned beets (⅛-inch strips)

2 tablespoons julienned dill pickles (⅛-inch strips)

Salt and freshly ground white pepper to taste

6 to 8 large leaves red leaf lettuce

18 to 24 black Greek olives, pitted

2 tomatoes, quartered

To prepare the dressing, place all the ingredients in a blender and blend for 30 seconds. Chill in the refrigerator.

To prepare the salad, wash the iceberg lettuce in ice water. Drain and spin dry using a salad spinner and place in a large wooden salad bowl. Add the ham, turkey, cheese, carrots, zucchini, beets, and pickles. Season with salt and pepper, add about 2 tablespoons of the dressing, and toss together, making sure the dressing is distributed evenly (add more dressing, if desired).

To serve, place a leaf of red leaf lettuce on each serving plate, mound the tossed salad on top of the leaf, and garnish with the olives and tomato quarters. Serve additional dressing on the side.

CHEF'S NOTES: The original recipe for Green Goddess dressing was created in the 1920s at the Palace Hotel in San Francisco (now called the Sheraton-Palace). The story goes that the hotel chef named the dressing for an actor who stayed there while performing in a play called *The Green Goddess.* The play was a Broadway hit and later became one of the first talkie movies in the early 1930s.

The julienned ingredients should be about 2 inches long and ¹/₈ inch wide.

The dressing recipe makes 2¹/₂ cups, which is sufficient for two salads. Reserve the remaining dressing in the refrigerator for another use; it will keep for up to 1 week.

SERVES: 6 TO 8

SIMPLICITY: + + +

MADISON AVENUE SALAD
with Creamy Roquefort Dressing

Neiman Marcus has served its own version of the classic Cobb salad for years. It was inspired by an article written by James Villas that I read several years ago (Villas is the author of the acclaimed cookbook My Mother's Southern Kitchen, *among others). He described how, in his "younger and overindulgent days," nothing gave him greater pleasure than partaking every Wednesday of the copious chicken salad lunch at the New York Plaza Hotel's Oak Bar, in those days a sophisticated bastion of male-only dining. First, he would enjoy two ice-cold, very dry martinis, allowing them "to work their magic on the soul." Then, he would linger over the Plaza's version of Cobb salad served with a velvety Roquefort dressing, washed down with a stein of draft English ale. I enjoyed reading the author's vivid food memory, and while I hesitate to recommend the liquid accompaniments, I have always kept the combination of ingredients in mind because they sounded so darned good! This is popular whenever we feature it on the Neiman Marcus menu, and we gave it the name because some of the best places to find a chopped salad in New York City happen to be located in Midtown on Madison Avenue.*

FOR THE CREAMY ROQUEFORT DRESSING

1 pound good-quality Roquefort cheese

½ cup sour cream

½ cup mayonnaise

¼ cup cider vinegar

¼ cup extra-virgin olive oil

¼ cup half-and-half

1 teaspoon minced shallot

1 teaspoon Worcestershire sauce

Salt and freshly ground white pepper to taste

FOR THE CHICKEN

3 whole double chicken breasts, bone in, skin on, about 1¼ pounds each

1 large carrot, peeled and diced

1 large onion, diced

1 celery stalk, diced

1 small bunch fresh parsley

3 sprigs fresh thyme

½ teaspoon white peppercorns

FOR THE SALAD

6 bacon slices, chopped

1 large head chicory or frisée, chopped

1 head romaine, chopped

1 large head radicchio, chopped, or 2 cups chopped red cabbage

6 deviled eggs (My Mother's Version, page 68), cut in half lengthwise

2 avocados, halved, pitted, peeled, and sliced

12 cherry tomatoes, halved, for garnish

To prepare the dressing, place the Roquefort in a bowl and lightly mash with a whisk. Add the cream, mayonnaise, vinegar, olive oil, half-and-half, shallot, and Worcestershire sauce and season with salt and pepper. Combine thoroughly; if the dressing seems too thick, add a little more half-and-half. Let the dressing sit in the refrigerator, covered, for at least 1 hour before serving to allow the flavors to marry.

To prepare the chicken, place the breasts in a large saucepan and add enough water to cover them by 2 inches. Bring to a boil and skim the surface with a large spoon to remove any floating fat or scum. Reduce the heat to a low simmer and add the carrot, onion, celery, parsley, thyme, and peppercorns. Simmer for 1 hour, skimming the surface occasionally. Remove the cooked chicken from the saucepan and cool. Cut the meat from the bones and dice.

To prepare the salad, place the bacon in a skillet and set over medium heat. Cook for 5 or 6 minutes, until crisp. Drain the bacon on paper towels and set aside. Place the chicory, romaine, and radicchio in a large wooden salad bowl and add 1 cup of the dressing; toss thoroughly to combine. To serve, arrange the tossed lettuces on serving plates and arrange 2 deviled egg halves to one side of each serving. Evenly divide the diced chicken among the plates and top with the avocado, cherry tomatoes, and bacon.

CHEF'S NOTE: The dressing recipe makes about 1½ cups and can be held in the refrigerator, covered tightly, for up to 1 week.

SERVES: 6

SIMPLICITY: ✦ ✦ ✦

HEARTS OF PALM SALAD
with Red French Dressing

At Neiman Marcus, we mostly serve this attractive salad for special springtime occasions, such as Easter and Mother's Day. Hearts of palm are harvested from the sabal palmetto, a tall palm originally known as "swamp cabbage" that is the state tree of Florida. Over recent years, recognition by chefs of the tenderness and delicate flavor of the core of the palm has led to its new nickname: millionaire's salad. Now listed as an endangered species in Florida, the palm is an important cash crop in South America, particularly Brazil.

FOR THE RED FRENCH DRESSING

2 tablespoons Tomato Ketchup (page 275) or
   store-bought ketchup

2 teaspoons kosher salt

1 teaspoon paprika

1 teaspoon sugar

1 garlic clove, minced

½ teaspoon dry mustard

Dash of Tabasco sauce

Dash of Worcestershire sauce

¼ cup red wine vinegar

1 cup vegetable oil

FOR THE SALAD

2 jars (14 ounces each) hearts of palm, drained

4 large handfuls of arugula (about 4 ounces)

12 to 16 cherry tomatoes, halved

1 small red onion, finely sliced

1 head Belgian endive, core removed and leaves
   pulled apart

Salt and freshly ground white pepper to taste

8 ounces thinly sliced Serrano ham or baked
   Virginia ham (12 to 16 thin slices)

1 cup shaved Parmesan cheese

To prepare the dressing, place the ketchup in a bowl and add the salt, paprika, sugar, garlic, mustard, Tabasco, and Worcestershire sauce. Stir in the vinegar, then pour in the oil in a slow, steady stream while whisking vigorously with a wire whisk. Whisk again before serving.

To prepare the salad, cut the hearts of palm in half on the bias and place in a large wooden salad bowl. Add the arugula, tomatoes, onion, and endive. Add 2 tablespoons of the dressing, season lightly with salt and pepper, and toss together. Remove the endive leaves and arrange around each serving plate. Top with the arugula and scatter the tomatoes, hearts of palm, and onion around each plate. Drape the ham over the arugula and sprinkle each salad with the Parmesan. Serve additional dressing on the side.

CHEF'S NOTES: Hearts of palm are a healthful food; they are high in fiber and low in fat and calories and contain no cholesterol. The dressing will keep in an airtight container in the refrigerator for up to 2 weeks.

SERVES: 6 TO 8

SIMPLICITY: + +

NEIMAN MARCUS FRUIT SALAD IN A MELON BASKET
with Poppy Seed Dressing

This recipe is all about the striking presentation. Since the early days of my hotel kitchen career, I have enjoyed cutting fruit to resemble flowers to garnish salads with a special flourish. This recipe will show you how to give simple fruit salad a five-star appearance. Choose whatever fruit is in season—summer watermelon and strawberries, fall apples and grapes—and be creative!

FOR THE POPPY SEED DRESSING

½ cup sugar

1 teaspoon dry mustard, such as Colman's

1 teaspoon kosher salt

6 tablespoons white wine vinegar

1 tablespoon grated onion, plus the juice released
    by grating

1 cup safflower or canola oil

1½ tablespoons poppy seeds

FOR THE FRUIT SALAD

4 cantaloupes

1 honeydew melon, peeled, seeded, and diced

3 fresh purple figs, quartered

6 black cherries

12 blackberries

2 tablespoons pomegranate seeds, for garnish

To prepare the dressing, place the sugar, mustard, salt, and vinegar in the bowl of an electric mixer. Add the grated onion and onion juice and mix on low speed. Turn the mixer to high and gradually add the oil in a steady stream until well incorporated. Continue to mix on high speed for 10 minutes longer, until the dressing is very thick. Stir in the poppy seeds, transfer the dressing to an airtight container, and reserve in the refrigerator.

To prepare the fruit salad, first make the melon baskets. Take 3 of the cantaloupe melons and use a sharp paring knife to make large *V*-shaped incisions into the circumference of the melons until the melons separate into 2 halves (see the photo on page 106). Cut off no more than about 1½ inches from the bottom of the melon halves so that they will stand flat. Still working on the rind side, use the knife to carefully make another incision in a *V*-shape about ¼ inch below the original *V*-shaped cuts, cutting just ½ inch into the flesh. Then, starting at the top point of each wedge,

cut downward into the wedge between the flesh and the rind. Gently pull the top edge of each point away from the flesh, forming a flower petal shape (see the photo on page 106).

Stand the remaining cantaloupe and the honeydew melon on a cutting board and peel away the rinds using a long paring knife. Cut the melons in half, remove the seeds, and then cut the flesh into small dice. Transfer to a bowl. Add the figs, cherries, and blackberries and mix gently. Spoon equal amounts of the fruit mixture into each melon basket and garnish with the pomegranate seeds. Serve the poppy seed dressing on the side.

CHEF'S NOTE: The dressing can be used on any salad containing fruit.

SERVES: 6

SIMPLICITY: + + + +

"SALAD MORE THAN"
with Orange Vinaigrette

It was Helen Corbitt who gave this recipe its quirky name, and it says a lot. I think the name reflects the fact that this salad is more like a main meal than a starter. With protein, vegetables, potatoes, and fruit, it certainly makes a filling lunchtime salad. Back in Helen's day, big salads like this one were less in fashion, so this was another area in which she was blazing new frontiers and setting trends.

FOR THE CHICKEN

3 whole chicken breasts, bone in, skin on, about
    1¼ pounds each

1 lemon, cut into 4 wedges

2 tablespoons olive oil

½ teaspoon dried oregano

4 sprigs fresh parsley, roughly chopped

½ teaspoon dried thyme

3 garlic cloves, crushed

Salt and coarsely ground black pepper to taste

FOR THE ORANGE VINAIGRETTE

¼ cup freshly squeezed orange juice

¼ cup cider vinegar

Juice of 1 lemon

Grated zest of 1 orange

½ cup olive oil

1 teaspoon minced fresh parsley

Salt and freshly ground white pepper to taste

FOR THE SALAD

1 pound fresh haricots verts, trimmed

1 pound small Red Bliss potatoes, cut into quarters

3 or 4 large tomatoes

Salt and freshly ground white pepper to taste

1 cup sliced celery

½ cup toasted sliced almonds (page 281)

3 oranges, peeled and sliced, for garnish

To prepare the chicken, place the breasts in a dish or a bowl and rub with the lemon wedges and olive oil. Season with the oregano, parsley, thyme, and garlic; cover and refrigerate for 1 hour.

Preheat the oven to 350°F.

Remove the chicken and transfer to a shallow roasting pan, skin side up. Season the skin well with the salt and pepper. Roast the chicken for about 45 minutes, or until cooked through. Remove from the oven and let cool. Once the chicken is cool to the touch, peel away the skin and remove the meat from the bones, leaving the breast meat intact. Cut the chicken breasts into slices and set aside in the refrigerator.

While the chicken is roasting, prepare the orange vinaigrette. Pour the orange juice, vinegar, and lemon juice into a bowl; add the orange zest and whisk together. Gradually whisk in the oil in a steady stream until thoroughly incorporated. Add the parsley, season with salt and pepper, and reserve in the refrigerator.

Prepare an ice bath by filling a large metal bowl with ice and water. Bring a saucepan of salted water to a boil and add the beans. Reduce the heat to a simmer and cook the beans for about 5 minutes, or until soft and tender. Use a slotted spoon or tongs to transfer the beans to the ice bath to stop the cooking process. Add the potatoes to the saucepan of boiling water and cook for about 12 minutes, until they are tender when pierced with a sharp knife. Drain in a colander and cool under cold running water. Set aside and let dry.

Cut the tomatoes in half using a *V* cut to create a star when finished (see photo). Set aside. Transfer the cooled beans and potatoes to a large wooden salad bowl, pour in ¼ cup of the vinaigrette, toss together to coat, and season with salt and pepper. Divide this mixture among the serving plates. In the same bowl, toss together the sliced chicken, the celery, almonds, and ¼ cup more of the vinaigrette. Place a tomato star on each plate next to the beans and potatoes and arrange the chicken salad on top of the tomato. Garnish each plate with 2 orange slices. Serve additional vinaigrette on the side.

CHEF'S NOTES: The chicken will yield about 2 pounds cooked chicken breast meat. The citrus vinaigrette goes well with any type of seafood salad, espccially salmon or shrimp, and with chicken salads. It will keep in the refrigerator, covered tightly, for up to I week.

SERVES: 6 TO 8

SIMPLICITY: + +

SPRING SALAD KILKENNY
with Creamy Herb Vinaigrette

Coinciding with Helen Corbitt's tenure in the kitchen at Neiman Marcus, "Fashion Fortnights" were introduced at the Dallas store—celebrations highlighting a particular country or region. During these two-week events, the store was suitably decorated, fashion shows and special events were held, and appropriate food was served in the Zodiac Room. Many countries were chosen over the years, including France, Britain, and Italy—and this recipe comes from the Irish Fortnight held in the mid-1970s. Its heritage appeals to me, of course, and it caught my eye because this style of iceberg wedge salad is making a comeback.

FOR THE CREAMY HERB VINAIGRETTE

¼ cup sour cream

½ cup mayonnaise

2 tablespoons white wine vinegar

2 teaspoons Dijon mustard

⅛ teaspoon garlic powder

1 teaspoon dried tarragon

1 teaspoon dried parsley

½ teaspoon sugar

Salt and freshly ground white pepper to taste

FOR THE SPRING SALAD

2 cucumbers, peeled, halved lengthwise, and
    seeded

1 small red onion, halved and thinly sliced

1 tablespoon kosher salt

3 bunches watercress, thick stems removed
    (about 3 cups)

1 cup thinly sliced radishes

1 head iceberg lettuce, cut into 6 or 8 wedges

6 to 8 cherry tomatoes, halved, for garnish

6 bacon slices, cooked and crumbled,
    for garnish

To prepare the vinaigrette, place all the ingredients in a small bowl, stir to combine thoroughly, and keep refrigerated.

To prepare the salad, cut the cucumber halves into half-moons and place in a wooden bowl. Add the onion and salt, toss thoroughly to combine, and marinate in the refrigerator for 2 hours. Taste the cucumbers; if they seem too salty, rinse the marinated vegetables under cold running water; drain very well. Transfer to a large wooden salad bowl, add the watercress, radishes, and ⅓ cup of the vinaigrette, and toss together to combine thoroughly. Place an iceberg lettuce wedge on each salad plate, cut side down, and drizzle about 2 teaspoons of the vinaigrette over each wedge. Arrange a small mound of the tossed salad over the wedge and garnish each plate with tomato halves and crumbled bacon.

CHEF'S NOTE: I improved on Helen Corbitt's recipe by salting the cucumber and onions to extract the moisture and soften them. After the salt is rinsed off, their texture is pliable but still crunchy—simply delicious.

SERVES: 6 TO 8

SIMPLICITY: + +

THE HIRSCHES' SUNDAY SALAD
with JG House Vinaigrette

When I think of Sunday meals, I always think of family and how eagerly we anticipated Sunday brunch or dinner at our house. Our corporate chef, Anita Hirsch, shared with me the Sunday lunchtime meal she loved best when she was young. After she and her siblings returned from Sunday school and her dad, Lou, returned from bowling with the guys, her mom would tackle the refrigerator and throw together a great bowl of greens and veggies that pleased the entire family. Moms of the 1950s and '60s didn't have the convenience of prepared salad dressings, so they created their own. Anita's mom used a mix of dried spices, a splash of red wine vinegar, and vegetable oil. In this recipe, I borrowed my wife Jody's vinaigrette recipe, which you will usually find at the Garvin house. Enjoy!

FOR THE JG HOUSE VINAIGRETTE

1 chicken bouillon cube

¼ teaspoon sugar

½ teaspoon freshly ground black pepper

¼ teaspoon garlic powder

¼ cup cider vinegar

¾ cup olive oil

FOR THE SUNDAY SALAD

3 new potatoes

1 teaspoon kosher salt

2 cans (6 ounces each) albacore tuna
    (all white meat)

3 hard-cooked eggs, cut into wedges

½ head iceberg lettuce, diced

½ head romaine lettuce, diced

1 large carrot, peeled and cut into ¼-inch slices

1 celery stalk, cut into ¼-inch slices

1 red bell pepper, seeded and diced

1 large tomato, diced

3 radishes, sliced

2 scallions, thinly sliced

3 anchovies, chopped

1 cup sliced pitted black olives

Freshly ground black pepper to taste

To prepare the vinaigrette, place the bouillon cube in a bowl containing 2 tablespoons water. Microwave on high for 30 seconds to dissolve the bouillon. Place the sugar in a bowl and add the pepper, garlic powder, and vinegar. Stir together and then let steep for 5 minutes. Whisk in the dissolved bouillon and gradually add the oil in a slow, steady stream while whisking vigorously. Whisk again before serving.

To prepare the salad, place the potatoes in a small saucepan, cover with water, and add the salt. Bring to a boil and simmer for 30 minutes, or until tender. Drain and let cool before cutting into small wedges; transfer to a large wooden salad bowl. Add all the remaining salad ingredients and ½ cup of the vinaigrette. Toss well and divide among the serving plates. Serve additional vinaigrette on the side.

CHEF'S NOTES: Serve with Garlic Toast (page 280). You can spiff up the dressing by adding any combination of chopped fresh herbs, capers, chopped pimientos, and a dash of Worcestershire or Tabasco sauce.

SERVES: 6 TO 8

SIMPLICITY: + +

fish and seafood

SEAFOOD CREPES
with Lobster and Shrimp

RED SNAPPER ESCABÈCHE

TEMPURA HADDOCK FILLETS
and Oven-Fried Potatoes

BBQ SEA SCALLOPS
with Lemon-Aïoli Dipping Sauce

STUFFED FLOUNDER
with Deviled Crab

FRIDAY NIGHT FOIL-ROASTED SALMON
with Rémoulade

ROASTED JUMBO SHRIMP LORENZO
with Crabmeat

LOBSTER MACARONI AND CHEESE

SOME OF MY earliest memories, from growing up in Philadelphia, are of going to "the shore" and summer months spent on the beach. These were great times for me and my family, and eating fresh seafood was always a highlight. Over the years, I have heard many food lovers lament that they never really had the chance to enjoy fresh seafood as they lived in a land-locked state far from any ocean. The fish at their local grocery store came frozen or was of doubtful vintage and provenance. The good news is that over the past fifteen years or so, we have seen food stores take advantage of changing consumer demand and palates; they have begun flying in fresh seafood from the U.S. coasts and beyond. Today, most people can get fresh fish and seafood at their local market anywhere in the country. More important, they can feel safer than ever that the fish has arrived from the supplier within a matter of days, and that it has been stored and handled in a proper manner.

From personal experience, I know that the ever-improving knowledge and expertise of suppliers and shippers mean the quality of fish and seafood has never been better. Don't be afraid to ask your seafood source about where a product comes from, whether it is fresh or has been frozen, and for recommendations. If the fish is not packaged, give it a good sniff; it should not smell fishy. Some people shy away from buying fish because of the odors left after cooking, but if you are sure the product is fresh, this will not be a problem. Ideally, inspect the whole fresh fish; it should have a uniform color and appear shiny, not dull, and should be blemish-free. The eyes should appear clear, not cloudy or sunken, and the gills should be bright red. If you press the flesh of the fish lightly, it should spring back and not stay depressed. If the fish does not satisfy these criteria, move along. Wait patiently for another shipment, or try another source.

Despite the encouraging trends in the supply of fish and seafood, many people do not know how to handle and cook it, or do not yet feel confident about doing so. With this in mind, I have chosen recipes for this chapter both from Helen Corbitt's archive and my own repertoire that are easy to prepare and tasty on the palate. I hope some of them become mainstays in your kitchen.

SEAFOOD CREPES
with Lobster and Shrimp

Crepes are a comfort food, and yet they are rarely made at home. When I joined Neiman Marcus in the mid-1990s, I was surprised to find them on the menu, as I considered crepes a little out of date. However, they were still popular with our guests, so I worked to update them; all these years later, crepes are back in vogue, and these especially—the combination of lobster and shrimp is hard to dislike! In fact, this is the single best-selling item whenever we add it to our menus. Chicken crepes and vegetable crepes make occasional appearances on our menus at Neiman Marcus as well.

FOR THE SHRIMP AND LOBSTER FILLING

2 tablespoons unsalted butter

1 shallot, minced

2 cups chopped white mushrooms

8 jumbo shrimp (about 12 ounces), peeled, deveined, and diced

1½ pounds cooked lobster (page 130), diced

4 cups warm Velouté (page 278)

2 tablespoons chopped fresh parsley

½ cup plus 2 tablespoons grated Parmesan cheese

1 cup diced fresh white bread, crust removed

Salt and freshly ground white pepper to taste

FOR THE CREPES

¾ cup all-purpose flour

⅛ teaspoon kosher salt

3 large eggs

2 tablespoons unsalted butter, melted, plus additional for sautéeing

1½ cups milk

To prepare the filling, place the butter in a heavy skillet and melt over medium-low heat. When the butter begins to bubble and sizzle, add the shallot and mushrooms and sauté for 3 to 4 minutes, until softened. Add the shrimp and cook for 4 or 5 minutes longer. Remove the skillet from the heat and stir in the cooked lobster, 2 cups of the warm velouté, 1 tablespoon of the parsley, ½ cup of the cheese, and the bread; season with salt and pepper. Set aside to cool.

To prepare the crepes, sift the flour and salt into a bowl. Using a whisk, beat in the eggs until the mixture is smooth and free of lumps. Stir in the butter and milk and then let the batter rest for 1 hour. Lightly butter a 5-inch nonstick skillet or crepe pan and set over medium heat. Pour in 2 tablespoons of the batter, or enough to coat the bottom of the pan evenly. Cook the crepe for about 1 minute, until the bottom is browned, and then flip it over and brown the other side. Repeat with the remaining batter; stack the crepes as they are made, separating them with parchment paper to keep them moist.

Place a crepe on a work surface on top of a piece of plastic wrap. Spoon about ¾ cup filling into the center of the crepe and then fold it up into an envelope shape or bundle. Wrap the filled crepe with the plastic wrap. Repeat with the remaining crepes and filling and keep refrigerated until ready to serve.

Rewarm the remaining 2 cups velouté in a saucepan. To serve, place 3 or 4 filled crepes at a time on a plate and reheat for 45 seconds to 1 minute in the microwave on high. Remove the plastic and set in the middle of a serving plate. Pour warm velouté over each crepe just before serving. Sprinkle with the remaining 1 tablespoon parsley and 2 tablespoons Parmesan cheese.

CHEF'S NOTES: You will need 3 lobsters (1¾ to 2 pounds) to yield the 1½ pounds cooked meat called for in this recipe. This is a good recipe for entertaining, as the crepes can be prepared ahead of time and then stored in the refrigerator before being microwaved.

SERVES: 6 TO 8

SIMPLICITY: ✦ ✦ ✦ ✦

RED SNAPPER ESCABÈCHE

The term **escabèche** *refers to the Spanish tradition of marinating ingredients such as fish, seafood, poultry, and vegetables in a spicy pickling liquid or sauce. Sometimes the technique is used to add flavor, and sometimes it is a means of preserving food. Because an escabèche marinade contains an acidic element such as vinegar or citrus juice, it "cooks" the main ingredient—a concept that intrigued me when I first tried it. Helen Corbitt prepared scallops this way at Neiman Marcus long before escabèche dishes (or the closely related seafood ceviches) became widely known to an American audience. In this dish, you can substitute scallops, grouper, halibut, or sea bass for the snapper.*

6 red snapper fillets, about 6 ounces each

Salt and freshly ground white pepper to taste

1 cup olive oil

½ cup thinly sliced carrots

½ cup seeded and thinly sliced red bell pepper

½ cup seeded and thinly sliced yellow bell pepper

½ cup seeded and thinly sliced poblano chile

1 jalapeño, cut in half and seeded

½ cup thinly sliced red onion

1 teaspoon ground coriander

6 sprigs fresh thyme

½ cup chopped fresh cilantro

1 cup white wine vinegar

1 lemon, thinly sliced

Season the snapper with salt and pepper. Pour ¼ cup of the olive oil into a large, heavy skillet set over medium-high heat and sauté the snapper for 2 minutes on each side, or until lightly browned. Transfer the fillets to a large casserole dish. Add ¼ cup more oil to the skillet and add the carrots, red and yellow bell peppers, poblano, jalapeño, and red onion. Stir together over medium-high heat and add the coriander, thyme, and cilantro. Sauté for 1 minute and season again with salt and pepper. Pour the vinegar into the skillet, add the lemon slices and the remaining ½ cup olive oil, and bring to a simmer. Remove from the heat and pour the escabèche mixture over the fish. Cover and transfer to the refrigerator; marinate for 24 hours before serving.

To serve, remove the snapper fillets from the marinade and transfer to a serving dish. Spoon the vegetables and a little of the marinade over the fish.

CHEF'S NOTES: This is a great dish to prepare for a large party because it is made in advance and guests can serve themselves. The neatly cut, colorful vegetables make for an attractive presentation.

SERVES: 6

SIMPLICITY: + + +

TEMPURA HADDOCK FILLETS
and Oven-Fried Potatoes

British Fortnight at Neiman Marcus was celebrated in the Zodiac restaurant with many great recipes, including one for outstanding fish and chips. Over the years, I have experienced many memorable versions of the British classic, but none has inspired me more than the Asian spin this recipe offers. I use haddock, the fish used for classic fish 'n' chips, but you can substitute fresh grouper, sole, or snapper fillet.

FOR THE ASIAN DIPPING SAUCE

1 cup unseasoned rice wine vinegar

1 tablespoon Asian fish sauce

1 tablespoon soy sauce

1 teaspoon sugar

2 scallions, thinly sliced

¼ teaspoon dried red pepper flakes

FOR THE TEMPURA BATTER

¾ cup all-purpose flour

½ cup cornstarch

1 teaspoon ground ginger

1 teaspoon baking powder

1½ cups (12 ounces) ale or dark beer, such as Bass

4 large eggs, separated

2 tablespoons olive oil

1 teaspoon soy sauce

8 haddock fillets, about 6 ounces each

Oven-Fried Potatoes (page 208)

To prepare the dipping sauce, mix all the ingredients together in a small bowl and chill in the refrigerator for at least 1 hour before serving.

To prepare the batter, place ½ cup of the flour and the cornstarch in a bowl and combine with the ginger and baking powder. Using your fingers to mix the dry ingredients, slowly add the beer to the bowl. Work the ingredients through your fingers until the mixture becomes a smooth paste. Whisk the egg yolks until creamy. Place the whites in a separate bowl, whisk until soft peaks form, and set aside. Add the yolks to the batter and, using a whisk, add the olive oil and soy sauce. Whisk in the egg whites and then let the batter sit for 1 hour to set up before beginning to fry.

Heat a deep fryer to 350°F. (Alternatively, heat 3 or 4 inches of vegetable oil in a large, heavy saucepan.)

Place the remaining ¼ cup flour on a plate and dredge the haddock in it. Dip the haddock into the batter and, using tongs, carefully place 2 or 3 of the haddock fillets into the deep fryer. Cook for 6 to 8 minutes, or until the fish is browned evenly; remove with a slotted spoon and drain on paper towels. Repeat for the remaining fillets. Serve with the fries and the dipping sauce.

CHEF'S NOTES: Haddock is closely related to cod, and it is always moist, making it relatively easy to cook; its flakiness makes for a great texture. The secret of getting lumps out of the tempura batter is to use your fingers; using a whisk gives inferior results.

SERVES: 8

SIMPLICITY: + + + +

BBQ SEA SCALLOPS
with Lemon-Aïoli Dipping Sauce

Don't let the name confuse you; while the scallops in this recipe **can** *easily be grilled in the backyard, we pan-sauté them in our (indoor) kitchen. The reason is that I like to control the heat and allow the sugars in the sauce to caramelize slowly and crisp the scallops perfectly. Only after the scallops are cooked do I skewer them to make them look grilled. (Even if you don't skewer them, they'll taste just fine.) The ideal accompaniment for this dish is the New England Cabbage Salad (page 187).*

FOR THE LEMON AÏOLI

3 large egg yolks

1 garlic clove, minced

1 teaspoon Dijon mustard

Juice of 1 lemon

1 cup vegetable oil

Salt and freshly ground white pepper to taste

FOR THE SCALLOPS

18 to 24 sea scallops (about 2 pounds), washed
   and patted dry

1 cup BBQ Sauce (page 271)

Salt and freshly ground white pepper to taste

2 tablespoons olive oil

To prepare the aïoli, place the egg yolks in a stainless-steel bowl and add the garlic, mustard, and half of the lemon juice. Using a wire whisk, add the oil in a slow, steady stream while whisking vigorously, stopping occasionally to scrape down the sides of the bowl. Whisk in the remaining lemon juice and season with salt and pepper. Transfer to an airtight container and refrigerate.

To prepare the scallops, place them in a large baking dish or casserole and add the BBQ sauce. Season with salt and pepper and cover the dish with plastic wrap. Transfer to the refrigerator and let marinate for 2 hours, turning the scallops once or twice.

To serve, pour the oil into a large nonstick skillet and set over medium-low heat. Add the marinated scallops a few at a time so as not to overcrowd the pan. Sauté on the first side for about 2 minutes, or until the sides are browned. Turn the scallops over and sauté for about 30 seconds longer. Remove the scallops and thread a skewer through each. Place 3 or 4 skewered scallops on each serving plate and serve with the aïoli.

CHEF'S NOTES: Buy dry-packed, unfrozen scallops for this dish—they are packed in their own juice, not in water. Otherwise, results will be less than perfect because frozen scallops will release the water they hold during the cooking process, making them tough. Large scallops (fewer than 10 to the pound) can be impressive just because of their size. Seek out a good-quality (and preferably local) fishmonger and ask him to order fresh scallops for you.

SERVES: 6 TO 8

SIMPLICITY: + +

STUFFED FLOUNDER
with Deviled Crab

You will find a dish similar to this one on the menu of most good seafood restaurants up and down the East Coast, and during my first kitchen job at Watson's restaurant in Ocean City, New Jersey, I seemed to be stuffing flounder all day long! Maybe that's why this recipe is so evocative of the seaside in summertime, and if I am anywhere near the beach, I will still try to track down crab-stuffed fish. Serve the stuffed flounder with baked potatoes; the Stuffed Twice-Baked Potatoes on page 207 are the perfect accompaniment.

3 tablespoons unsalted butter, plus additional
    for the casserole dish

1 small onion, finely diced

1 green bell pepper, finely diced

1 pound jumbo lump crabmeat

6 sprigs fresh parsley, chopped

1 teaspoon Dijon mustard

2 slices white sandwich bread (crusts removed),
    coarsely diced

½ cup mayonnaise

1 teaspoon Worcestershire sauce

¼ teaspoon Tabasco sauce

2 large eggs

Salt and freshly ground white pepper to taste

6 to 8 skinless flounder fillets, about 7 ounces
    each

1 lemon, cut into small pieces

½ cup dry white wine

1 tablespoon paprika

Preheat the oven to 350°F. Butter a large ovenproof casserole dish.

Melt 1 tablespoon of the butter in a skillet over medium heat and sauté the onion and bell pepper for 3 minutes until softened. Remove the skillet from the heat and let cool. In a large bowl, combine the crabmeat, the cooled onion mixture, the parsley, mustard, bread, mayonnaise, Worcestershire sauce, Tabasco, and eggs. Mix carefully to avoid breaking up the crabmeat too much and season with salt and pepper.

Lay the fillets on a large cutting board, flat side (former skin side) up. Season the top of each fillet with salt and pepper and place equal amounts of the crab stuffing on each fillet before rolling them up. Arrange the rolled-up fillets in the prepared casserole, seam side down. Squeeze the lemon pieces over the fish to release the juice and place the squeezed lemon directly on top of the rolls. Pour the white wine over the fish and dot the fillets with the remaining 2 tablespoons butter. Sprinkle the paprika

over the fillets and cover the casserole with foil. Bake for 30 minutes, then remove the foil and bake for 20 minutes longer, or until the filling is bubbly and beginning to brown. Remove the fillets from the oven and let cool for 5 minutes before serving.

CHEF'S NOTE: The crab stuffing in this recipe also works well as a crab cake recipe. Just form into patties, lightly flour, and pan-fry in a little vegetable oil or butter until cooked through.

SERVES: 6 TO 8

SIMPLICITY: + + +

FRIDAY NIGHT FOIL-ROASTED SALMON

with Rémoulade

Like many Catholic families, mine ate fish every Friday night—never red meat. My mother, who was an excellent cook, loved how easy this recipe was to prepare and how well it kept in the refrigerator for a few hours until she was ready to bake it. Bluefish was another Friday night favorite, and kingfish if a relative caught some. This recipe can be used for fillets of almost any large fish that has a high fat content, such as grouper, sea bass, and snapper; do not try it with tuna, swordfish, or flatfish such as flounder or sole, as they are not suited to this cooking method.

FOR THE RÉMOULADE

1 cup mayonnaise

3 anchovies, minced

½ tablespoon capers, rinsed

2 sprigs minced fresh parsley

½ teaspoon Dijon mustard

½ tablespoon minced fresh tarragon

½ teaspoon minced dill pickle

Juice of ½ lemon

Salt and freshly ground white pepper to taste

FOR THE SALMON

1 side of salmon (2 to 2½ pounds)

¼ cup mayonnaise

1 onion, thinly sliced

5 sprigs fresh thyme

5 sprigs fresh tarragon

1 lemon, thinly sliced

Salt and freshly ground white pepper to taste

⅛ teaspoon cayenne pepper

2 tablespoons unsalted butter, cut into small
   pieces

¼ cup dry white wine

Place all of the rémoulade ingredients in a bowl, combine thoroughly, and chill in the refrigerator for at least 30 minutes before serving.

Preheat the oven to 350°F.

Tear off a 24-inch-long piece of kitchen foil and lay it on a baking sheet. Place the salmon fillet on the foil and spread the mayonnaise over the entire surface of the fish. Scatter the onion, thyme, tarragon, and lemon slices over the mayonnaise and season with the salt, pepper, and cayenne. Scatter the butter over the fish and then pour the white wine over, pinching up the edges of the foil so the wine does not leak out. Fold the foil over to form a loose tent and pinch again gently to seal the foil package. Transfer the salmon to the oven and roast for 30 minutes. Open the foil carefully, avoiding the hot steam that will escape. Check the doneness of the fish by inserting the tip of a small knife into the flesh to see if it is cooked all the way through. Pour off the liquid from the foil into a small bowl so it can be served with the fish. Use a spatula to portion the fish pieces for your guests; pour the reserved juice over each portion before serving with the rémoulade.

CHEF'S NOTES: This recipe also works well on the grill. Just lay the foil-wrapped fish over medium heat and "bake" for 20 to 25 minutes. Good accompaniments for the salmon are simple boiled potatoes and fresh peas or spinach.

SERVES: 6 TO 8

SIMPLICITY: + +

ROASTED JUMBO SHRIMP LORENZO
with Crabmeat

I created this version of shrimp Lorenzo when I was working at the Sheraton Denver Tech Center in Colorado, and it's as good now as it ever was. The secret ingredient is Pernod, the French liqueur with a licorice flavor; I had just discovered it and was experimenting with how best to match its distinctive tones. Snow crab is less expensive than blue crab, king crab, or Dungeness crab, which can all be substituted, but you will need to squeeze the snow crab gently to remove excess moisture. I like to put this dish on the menu at Neiman Marcus during the holiday season, as it is a little indulgent and perfect for special occasions. Serve with a simple pasta, dressed with a little olive oil and garlic.

FOR THE CRABMEAT STUFFING

12 ounces fresh spinach, stemmed

2 tablespoons all-purpose flour

2 tablespoons unsalted butter, plus additional
    for the pan

1½ cups heavy cream

1 pound snow crabmeat

2 tablespoons Pernod

1 cup grated Parmesan cheese

1 teaspoon grated nutmeg

Salt and freshly ground white pepper to taste

Dash of Tabasco sauce

Dash of Worcestershire sauce

½ teaspoon garlic powder

FOR THE SHRIMP

18 to 24 jumbo shrimp (1½ to 2 pounds), peeled
    and deveined, tails left on

½ cup dry white wine

2 tablespoons olive oil

2 lemons, quartered

6 to 8 sprigs fresh parsley, for garnish

To prepare the stuffing, bring a small saucepan of water to a boil, add the spinach, and cook for 2 minutes. Drain the spinach, gently squeeze dry, and set aside. In a small bowl, mix the flour and butter together using your fingers (this mixture, used to thicken sauces, is called a *beurre manié* in classical French cuisine). Pour the cream into a small saucepan, bring to a boil, and remove the pan from the heat. Whisk in the beurre manié until the mixture has a thick consistency (similar to that of mashed potatoes).

In a large bowl, mix together the crab, cooked spinach, and cream sauce. Stir in the Pernod, fold in the Parmesan, and season with the nutmeg, salt, and pepper. Add the Tabasco, Worcestershire sauce, and garlic powder, stir together, and let the mixture sit for 30 minutes in the refrigerator so the flavors can marry.

Preheat the oven to 350°F. Butter a baking sheet or a roasting pan.

Using a small, sharp knife, deeply butterfly the shrimp by cutting them in half along the vein side while leaving the tail attached. Flatten out the shrimp and arrange cut side up on the prepared baking sheet. Place 1 heaping tablespoon crab mixture on top of each shrimp. Pour the white wine into the pan and drizzle the olive oil over the shrimp. Bake the shrimp for 12 minutes, or until they are no longer translucent. Transfer 3 or 4 shrimp to each serving plate, spritz with lemon, and garnish with the parsley.

CHEF'S NOTES: You can make the stuffing without the Pernod, but the flavor will not be the same if you leave it out. The stuffing freezes well, so leftovers can be used later to stuff chicken or as an omelet filling.

SERVES: 6 TO 8

SIMPLICITY: + + +

LOBSTER MACARONI AND CHEESE

Macaroni and cheese is an everyday favorite that everyone likes, so I enjoyed the challenge of dressing it up and making it even better. We serve this dish at many of our Neiman Marcus Cafés, and it has proved a huge success. Who would have thought that the humble mac 'n' cheese could be so elegant and refined, yet retain all its lovable qualities?

2 lemons, sliced

3 dried bay leaves

2 tablespoons black peppercorns

¼ cup kosher salt

2 live Maine lobsters, 1¾ to 2 pounds each

1 pound dried penne pasta

8 cups Velouté (page 278)

1 garlic clove, minced

2 sprigs fresh thyme

½ cup grated Parmesan cheese

½ cup grated Port Salut cheese

½ cup grated Gruyère cheese

½ cup grated Fontina cheese

Salt and freshly ground white pepper to taste

1 cup seasoned dry bread crumbs

To prepare the lobster, fill a stockpot with 6 quarts cold water and add the lemons, bay leaves, peppercorns, and salt. Cover and bring to a boil. Reduce the heat to medium-low and simmer for 15 minutes to flavor the poaching liquid. Add the lobsters, headfirst, cover the pot, and cook for about 10 minutes, or until the lobsters are bright red.

Prepare an ice bath in a large bowl. Using a pair of tongs, carefully remove the lobsters from the stockpot and transfer them to the ice bath to stop the cooking process. When the lobsters are cool enough to handle, remove the claws. Using a nutcracker, crack the shells and carefully remove the claw meat. Use a sharp knife to cut the claw meat in half lengthwise, removing any cartilage, and reserve the meat. Crack the first joint and carefully remove the knuckle meat; reserve. Cut the lobster bodies in half lengthwise, remove the tail meat, and cut it into several pieces along with the reserved claw and knuckle meat. Discard the shells or save for another use, such as

stock. Dice the lobster meat and reserve in the refrigerator (there should be about 1 pound cooked meat).

Bring a large saucepan of salted water to a boil. Add the pasta, cook according to the directions on the box (typically 8 to 10 minutes), and drain. Rinse under cold running water, drain again, and set aside.

Preheat the oven to 350°F. Lightly butter a 3-quart casserole dish or six to eight 6-ounce ovenproof ramekins.

Put the velouté sauce in a saucepan and set over medium-low heat. Whisking constantly, add the garlic, thyme, and all four cheeses. Season with salt and pepper and continue cooking for 2 minutes, or until the cheeses are melted. Reduce the heat to low and add the diced lobster meat and the cooked pasta. Mix thoroughly and check the seasoning. Remove the pan from the heat.

Transfer the cheese and lobster mixture to the prepared casserole and top with the bread crumbs. Bake for 20 minutes, or until the cheese sauce begins to bubble.

CHEF'S NOTES: The four cheeses in the sauce give the dish an appealing complexity. Note that you will need to factor up the velouté recipe 4 times, from 2 cups to the 8 cups needed here.

SERVES: 6 TO 8

SIMPLICITY: ✦ ✦ ✦

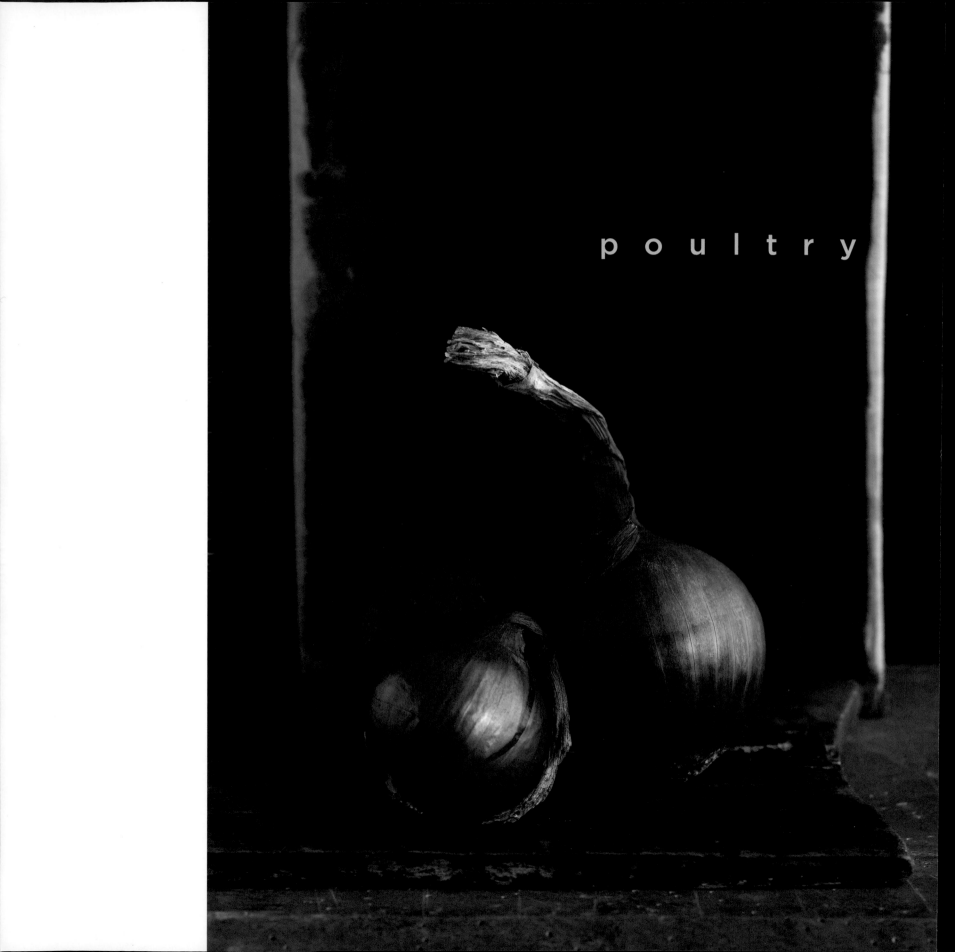

poultry

and game birds

BLACK-BOTTOM DUCK
with Pine Nut–Studded Wild Rice

OVEN-ROASTED STUFFED TURKEY
with Pan Gravy

CRISPY CHICKEN DRUMMERS
with Coleslaw

ROASTED GAME HENS
with Sauerkraut

ADOBO CHICKEN
with Stir-Fried Rice

WOK-SEARED MARINATED QUAIL
with Spicy Asian Noodles

CHICKEN TETRAZZINI

CHICKEN BREAST
Stuffed with Prosciutto, Fontina, and
Spinach à la Française

CREAMED CHICKEN À LA KING
in a Savory Parmesan Popover

"FAMILY MEAL" ROAST CHICKEN

OF ALL THE CHAPTERS in this book, this one was the quickest to pull together. One reason is that Neiman Marcus customers have always preferred this lean meat, and as I was shuffling through the many poultry recipes of Helen Corbitt, I noticed some favorites that are still bestsellers in our restaurants today. I have particularly enjoyed reworking her Chicken Tetrazzini recipe and her classic Chicken à la King, and even her take on fried chicken legs proved tasty and not at all outdated. There have been some changes, of course, in preferences and patterns as the American food revolution has developed over the last thirty years or so. We have seen an upsurge in demand for organic, free-range poultry and for antibiotic- and hormone-free meat, which is to be encouraged. These chickens may cost a little more, but the health benefits are proven and the flavor is invariably superior.

Having lived in Texas for the past twenty years, I've also been called upon to "fix" (as the Texans say) a variety of game birds. This means I have become a chef authority on duck, quail, and turkey, for example, and for that reason I decided to include recipes for each. While looking through Helen Corbitt's recipes, I became particularly excited about her Black-Bottom Duck recipe; the name appealed to me first, and then when I thought about the method she used of basting the duck continuously with a thick molasses-type marinade, I felt compelled to try it. Sure enough, the fabulous-looking lacquered duck came out perfectly. It's the chance to revive wonderful lost gems like this recipe that really gets my juices flowing, and those who have tasted it since I rediscovered Helen's dish have not been disappointed!

BLACK-BOTTOM DUCK
with Pine Nut–Studded Wild Rice

I love the name Helen Corbitt came up with for this dish, more commonly known these days as **lacquered duck.** *The best part of most roasts is the cooked-on bits left in the bottom of the pan mixed with the natural juices. Here, the pan juices mixed with a sweet, dark citrus sauce are basted over the bird, loading flavors back onto the skin and infusing the duck with those precious bastings. This is a truly outstanding dish, exciting to both the eye and the palate.*

¼ cup light brown sugar

2 tablespoons cider vinegar

½ cup freshly squeezed orange juice

1 cup dark molasses

3 ducks, 3 to 4 pounds each

Salt and coarsely ground black pepper to taste

3 large carrots, peeled and diced

2 onions, diced

3 celery stalks, sliced

3 garlic cloves, crushed

3 oranges, quartered

Pine Nut–Studded Wild Rice (page 212)

Preheat the oven to 425°F.

Place the brown sugar in a saucepan and stir in the vinegar, orange juice, and molasses. Set over medium heat and bring to a simmer. Remove the pan from the heat.

Season the cavities and skin of the ducks with salt and pepper. In a bowl, combine the carrots, onions, celery, garlic, and oranges. Fill the cavities with this mixture, squeezing the oranges as you insert them. Transfer 2 of the ducks to a roasting rack set inside a large roasting pan and place the third in another roasting pan. Roast in the oven, uncovered, for 15 minutes, then brush some of the basting sauce over the ducks. Repeat every 15 minutes (if the sauce is used up, use the pan drippings to baste every 15 minutes). After 45 minutes, reduce the oven temperature to 325°F. Cook for about 30 minutes longer, continuing to baste, or until the internal temperature reaches 165°F.

Transfer the ducks to a serving platter and let rest for 10 minutes; baste again before carving. Serve with the wild rice.

SERVES: 6

SIMPLICITY: + + +

OVEN-ROASTED STUFFED TURKEY

with Pan Gravy

On Thanksgiving Day, I begin preparations for the main meal as early as 7 A.M. I like to have everything well organized so the day runs smoothly, and that's the key to success. For those daunted by the enormity of the task, this recipe is a godsend. Fresh turkeys tend to be too dry, so buy a frozen bird and allow a couple of days for slow thawing in the refrigerator. There's a bonus to this recipe: You can use the carcass for the wonderful turkey soup recipe on page 62. Side dishes to consider with the turkey are Roasted Brussels Sprouts (page 177), Sweet Potato Pone (page 186), and Scalloped Potatoes (page 204).

1 turkey, about 14 pounds

FOR THE STUFFING

1½ cups Chicken Broth (page 267) or store-
    bought chicken stock

½ cup (1 stick) unsalted butter, chopped

1 onion, finely diced

2 celery stalks, finely diced

2 garlic cloves, crushed

1 tablespoon poultry seasoning

1 day-old French baguette, torn into pieces

½ cup milk

2 large eggs

Salt and freshly ground black pepper to taste

FOR THE TURKEY AND GRAVY

8½ cups Chicken Broth (page 267) or
    store-bought chicken stock

5 dried bay leaves

4 sprigs fresh thyme

1 cup kosher salt

Salt and freshly ground black pepper to taste

¼ cup (½ stick) softened unsalted butter

2 tablespoons olive oil

1 onion, diced

2 carrots, peeled and sliced

2 celery stalks, sliced

6 garlic cloves, sliced

FOR THE PAN GRAVY

6 tablespoons all-purpose flour

On the Monday night before Thanksgiving, place the frozen turkey in the refrigerator to begin thawing.

First thing on Thanksgiving morning, prepare the stuffing. Pour the chicken broth into a saucepan and bring to a simmer. Place the butter in a skillet or a sauté pan and melt over medium-high heat. Add the onion and celery and sauté for 2 minutes. Add the garlic and poultry seasoning and sauté for 2 minutes longer. Transfer to a bowl and add the warm chicken broth, torn bread, milk, and eggs. Mix well and season with salt and pepper; the stuffing should have a creamy texture. Let cool completely unless you are ready to stuff and roast your turkey immediately.

Preheat the oven to 350°F.

To prepare the turkey, rinse it well in the sink. Remove the giblet package and neck from the cavity (some turkeys also contain a gravy package; I'll have to admit I always throw away the gravy packet because something about a liquid frozen in a turkey cavity bothers me). Open the giblet package, discard the liver, and place the remaining contents in a small saucepan along with the neck. Add 2½ cups of the chicken broth, the bay leaves, and 1 sprig of thyme and bring to a simmer. Continue to gently simmer for 30 minutes and then remove from the heat. This mixture will be the basting liquid once you start roasting the turkey.

Meanwhile, after rinsing the turkey inside and out, fill the sink with water to cover the turkey and pour in the cup of kosher salt; let the bird rest in the salted water for 1 hour. Drain the water, but do not rinse the bird again. Season the turkey inside with salt and pepper before stuffing. Keep the turkey in the sink while filling the cavity with the stuffing (this makes cleanup easy); do not pack the bird too tightly. Transfer the stuffed turkey to a wire rack placed inside a large roasting pan. Rub the outside of the turkey with the softened butter and season again with a little salt and pepper. Pour the olive oil around the turkey and add the onion, carrots, celery, garlic, and remaining 3 thyme sprigs to the pan. Roast for about 4½ hours (allow about 20 minutes per pound). After the first hour, pour 1 cup of the reserved basting liquid over the bird and repeat 1 hour later (after that, there will be enough liquid in the pan to baste the bird every hour with its own juices). After about 2 hours, you may want to cover the turkey with foil if it is becoming too brown. After 3 hours of cooking, insert a meat thermometer into the turkey breast just above the spot where the wings attach. Remove the turkey from the oven when the internal temperature reaches 160°F.

When the turkey has finished roasting, remove it from the pan and set it on a large serving platter. Place the roasting pan on the stovetop over medium heat,

straddling 2 burners if necessary. Add the remaining 6 cups chicken broth and bring to a simmer. Deglaze the pan by scraping the bottom with a wooden spoon to loosen bits of turkey and vegetable that have become attached. In a bowl, mix the flour with 1½ cups water and stir to form a smooth paste (called whitewash). Whisk half of the whitewash into the simmering stock and, once incorporated, add the rest. The mixture will thicken; continue whisking for 5 minutes. If the gravy gets too thick, add a little more stock; if it seems too thin, add more whitewash. Strain the gravy through a medium strainer into a clean saucepan; check the seasoning, add more salt and pepper as necessary, and keep warm.

Carve the turkey. Remove the breast meat from the carcass by cutting down through the top of the bird, following the breast blade all the way down to where the wing meets the breast. Lay the boneless breast on a cutting board and carefully slice crosswise. Using your fin-

gers, remove the drumstick and thigh in one piece and separate into 2 portions with a knife. Slice the remaining dark meat from the carcass. Remove the stuffing to a serving bowl. Serve the turkey meat with the stuffing and gravy.

CHEF'S NOTES: Unless you plan ahead and have French bread that is a day or two old, begin preparing the baguette for the stuffing the night before Thanksgiving Day. Preheat the oven to 225°F, tear the bread into pieces, and place on a cookie sheet. Transfer to the oven, turn the oven off, and let sit overnight to dry.

If you have any stuffing that did not fit inside the turkey, butter a casserole dish and add the remaining stuffing. Bake in the oven at 350°F until the internal temperature reaches 160°F.

SERVES: 8

SIMPLICITY: + + +

CRISPY CHICKEN DRUMMERS
with Coleslaw

No cookbook with recipes from Texas or the South would be complete without a fried chicken recipe. Southern cooks have perfected the technique, and their secret is soaking the chicken in buttermilk, which helps the flour coating to adhere just right so it crisps nicely. This is Helen Corbitt's recipe, and her addition of celery seed and curry to the coating gives a familiar favorite an intriguing exotic twist; when your guests taste it for the first time, they will wonder what makes it taste so good. Texas Corn Bread (page 28) completes this dish perfectly.

18 chicken drumsticks

2 cups buttermilk

1½ cups all-purpose flour

¼ teaspoon garlic salt

¼ teaspoon freshly ground white pepper

¼ teaspoon celery seed

¼ teaspoon curry powder

Coleslaw (page 190)

Rinse the chicken pieces well and transfer them to a large dish or bowl. Pour in the buttermilk and let the drumsticks soak for 2 to 3 hours in the refrigerator.

Heat 2 quarts of vegetable oil in a deep fryer or a large saucepan to 350°F. Preheat the oven to 350°F.

In a large bowl, whisk together the flour, garlic salt, pepper, celery seed, and curry powder. Remove the chicken from the buttermilk and dredge in the flour mixture. Shake off any excess flour and transfer to the deep fryer. Cook for 6 to 8 minutes, or until golden brown. Remove with tongs and place the drumsticks in an ovenproof casserole dish. Transfer to the oven and bake for 15 minutes, or until the chicken juices run clear when the tip of a sharp knife is inserted into the thickest part of the drumstick.

Serve the chicken in a basket lined with wax paper with a heaping side of coleslaw served in a ramekin.

CHEF'S NOTES: You can make this recipe just as well with bone-in chicken thighs or breasts; just increase the baking time by 10 to 12 minutes. The chicken is finished in the oven because it is not fully cooked when the pieces reach the desired color during frying.

SERVES: 6

SIMPLICITY: + + +

ROASTED GAME HENS
with Sauerkraut

I am a huge fan of sauerkraut, a dish that originated in the Alsace region of France. Alsace has been occupied periodically by Germany over the centuries, hence the Germanic name. This recipe is a reworked version of a banquet dish I used to prepare years ago, and the beauty of the technique is that the whole birds caramelize and yield great flavor; they also retain plenty of moisture and natural juices. Even so, the cabbage is infused with their essences. Try serving this family-style for an impressive weekend dinner.

2 cups store-bought sauerkraut

2 slices bacon, chopped

1 small onion, finely diced

¼ cup dry white wine

1 tablespoon caraway seeds

4 tablespoons (½ stick) softened unsalted butter

1 cup pearl onions, peeled

2 garlic cloves

12 fingerling potatoes, cut in half on the bias

1 large carrot, peeled and diced

6 game hens, 12 ounces to 1 pound each

Salt and coarsely ground black pepper to taste

1½ cups dark beer

Rinse the sauerkraut in a colander under cold running water; drain and gently squeeze dry. Place the bacon in a large sauté pan and set over medium heat. Sauté for about 5 minutes, or until the bacon begins to brown, and then add the diced onion. Cook for 2 or 3 minutes longer. Add the wine and the drained sauerkraut and cook for 2 minutes longer. Add the caraway seeds, spread the sauerkraut in a large roasting pan, and set aside.

Preheat the oven to 425°F.

Place 2 tablespoons of the butter in a large sauté pan and melt over medium-high heat. Add the pearl onions, garlic, potatoes, and carrot and sauté for 7 to 10 minutes, or until they start to brown. Arrange the sautéed vegetables over the sauerkraut in the roasting pan.

Rub the skin of the game hens with the remaining 2 tablespoons butter and generously season both the cavities and skin of the birds with salt and pepper. Place the hens on top of the vegetables and sauerkraut in the roasting pan. Pour the beer into the sauté pan used to cook the vegetables and deglaze by scraping the bottom with a wooden spoon to loosen the solids that have become attached. Bring to a boil, cook for 2 minutes, and then pour the mixture around the game hens. Transfer to the oven and bake for 20 minutes, or until the hens begin to brown. Reduce the oven temperature to 350°F, cover the roasting pan with foil, and bake for 20 to 25 minutes longer, or until the juices run clear when the meat between the breast and the thigh is pierced with the tip of a sharp knife.

To serve, spoon some of the sauerkraut onto each serving plate and add the vegetables. Serve the game hens on top of the sauerkraut with some of the juice from the pan spooned over them.

CHEF'S NOTE: *Sauerkraut* literally means "sour cabbage" in German. If you have any sauerkraut left over, make sure you have some good-quality hot dogs or bratwurst on hand!

SERVES: 6

SIMPLICITY: + + +

ADOBO CHICKEN
with Stir-Fried Rice

This recipe entered my repertoire in the early days of my career during my stay on the Hawaiian island of Kauai. I worked there at the Waiohai ("why-o-high") Hotel under the tutelage of executive chef Uwe Henze, a friend of my family's from Philadelphia. There were a lot of Filipino cooks in the kitchen, and this dish was the staff meal we enjoyed in the cafeteria most days. When I cooked it at home for my family, it won rave reviews—so enthusiastic, in fact, that I decide every now and then to have our Neiman Marcus Cafés offer it as a special.

FOR THE CHICKEN ADOBO

3 tablespoons olive oil

6 chicken thighs, bone in, skin on

6 chicken drumsticks, bone in, skin on

2 pounds chicken breasts, bone in, skin on

12 garlic cloves

1 cup soy sauce

½ cup unseasoned rice wine vinegar

½ cup white vinegar

5 dried bay leaves

6 black peppercorns

FOR THE STIR-FRIED RICE

1½ cups rice

3 tablespoons sesame oil

3 tablespoons vegetable oil

2 large eggs, beaten

2 cups sliced cremini mushrooms

3 garlic cloves, crushed

2 cups sliced water chestnuts

1 bunch scallions, thinly sliced

1 teaspoon white sesame seeds

3 tablespoons soy sauce

Preheat the oven to 375°F.

To prepare the chicken, heat the olive oil in a large, heavy skillet over medium heat. Add the chicken pieces in batches and brown for 3 or 4 minutes on each side; transfer to a large ovenproof casserole dish. When all the chicken is browned, add the garlic to the skillet and sauté for about 2 minutes; add to the chicken pieces. Drain any remaining oil from the pan, return to medium heat, and add the soy sauce, rice wine vinegar, white vinegar, bay leaves, and peppercorns. Deglaze the skillet by scraping the bottom with a wooden spoon to loosen the solids. Bring to a boil and pour the mixture over the chicken. Transfer the chicken to the oven and bake, uncovered, for about 40 minutes, basting frequently. Finish by turning the oven to broil; broil the chicken for 2 to 3 minutes, until the skin begins to get crisp.

While the chicken bakes, prepare the rice: Pour 3 cups cold water into a saucepan and add the rice. Bring the water to a simmer, cover the pan, and reduce the heat to low. Continue to simmer for 15 to 20 minutes, or until all the liquid is absorbed. Remove from the heat and set aside. Pour 1 tablespoon each of the sesame oil and vegetable oil into a large, heavy skillet and set over medium heat. Add the eggs and scramble them; transfer to a small bowl and set aside. Add the remaining 2 tablespoons each sesame oil and vegetable oil to the skillet and set over medium-high heat. Add the mushrooms, garlic, and water chestnuts and sauté for 5 minutes. Add the scallions and sesame seeds and sauté for 1 minute longer. Add the cooked rice and the soy sauce, using a large wooden spoon to keep the rice moving while incorporating all the ingredients. Add the scrambled eggs and stir together.

Transfer the stir-fried rice to serving plates and top with the adobo chicken. Spoon some of the sauce from the chicken over each serving.

CHEF'S NOTE: Adobo is a popular preparation in the Philippines for pork and chicken. Typically, the meat is cooked slowly with a well-balanced blend of spices, vinegar, soy sauce, and garlic.

SERVES: 6

SIMPLICITY: + + +

Stanley Marcus congratulating Executive Chef André Papion upon completion of a 1957 Chevaliers du Tasterin dinner in the Dallas Zodiac Restaurant.

WOK-SEARED MARINATED QUAIL
with Spicy Asian Noodles

Wing shooting is a popular sport in the Lone Star State, and a cookbook from Texas would not be complete without a quail recipe! I know when hunting season is upon us because many of my friends and relatives bring me quail they have bagged. Over the years, I have learned two important things about cooking quail: Make sure all the buckshot is removed, and use a great marinade. This particular marinade also lends great flavor to most types of red meat.

½ cup soy sauce

2 tablespoons unseasoned rice wine vinegar

4 garlic cloves, crushed

2 tablespoons crushed fresh ginger

1 large shallot, minced

1 jalapeño, seeded and minced

2 teaspoons Chinese five-spice powder

5 tablespoons sesame oil

3 tablespoons vegetable oil

12 semi-boneless quail (see Chef's Note)

¼ cup sherry or red wine

1½ pounds linguine

To prepare the marinade, place the soy sauce and vinegar in a bowl and add the garlic, ginger, shallot, jalapeño, and five-spice powder. Mix well and then gradually whisk in 4 tablespoons of the sesame oil and 2 tablespoons of the vegetable oil in a steady stream until completely incorporated.

Place the quail in a large dish and pour half of the marinade over them (reserve the remainder for the noodles). Turn to coat, then cover and marinate in the refrigerator for up to 2 hours.

Preheat the oven to 350°F.

Pour the remaining 1 tablespoon each sesame oil and vegetable oil into a large skillet or a wok and set over medium heat. Remove the quail from the marinade and add to the skillet. Sear on all sides for 2 to 3 minutes, until browned, and then transfer to a shallow roasting pan. Deglaze the skillet by adding the sherry and scraping the bottom of the pan with a wooden spoon to loosen the solids. Pour the sherry mixture over the quail and transfer the roasting pan to the oven. Roast for 15 to 20 minutes and then check for doneness by inserting the tip of a sharp knife into the wing bone area; if the juices run clear, the quail are cooked.

While the quail are roasting, prepare the noodles. Bring a saucepan of salted water to a boil and add the linguine. Cook as directed on the package; typically, linguine takes 8 to 10 minutes to cook al dente. Drain the linguine (do not rinse under running water) and place in a serving bowl. Add the reserved marinade and toss to combine.

Transfer the quail to serving plates; if there are any drippings left in the pan, pour over the quail. Serve with the noodles.

CHEF'S NOTE: Store-bought semi-boneless quail, as the name suggests, have had most of the bones removed by machine; only the wing bones and drumettes remain, making them much easier to eat.

SERVES: 6

SIMPLICITY: + + +

CHICKEN TETRAZZINI

This dish, which originated in San Francisco in the early 1900s, was named after the famous opera star Luisa Tetrazzini. That said, the exact origins of the dish and its composition are somewhat hazy, and several similar versions of the recipe exist. Luisa Tetrazzini was born in Florence and enjoyed a successful and sometimes spectacular operatic career, eclipsed only by Dame Nellie Melba, with whom she had a bitter feud. The story goes that at the time she made San Francisco her home, Tetrazzini encountered contractual difficulties that prevented her from performing. She famously declared, "I will sing in San Francisco if I have to sing there in the streets, for I know the streets of San Francisco are free." After winning her legal case, she announced she would indeed sing there in public, and on Christmas Eve in 1910 she serenaded her adopted city on a stage set up on the corner of Market Street and Kearney; her audience was an estimated 250,000 fans. In gratitude, a city restaurant named a chicken creation after the chanteuse.

2 tablespoons olive oil

6 boneless, skinless chicken breasts, about 6 ounces each

Salt and freshly ground white pepper to taste

1 pound linguine

1 teaspoon minced garlic

2 cups sliced button mushrooms

¼ cup dry white wine

2 cups warm Velouté (page 278)

2 cups heavy cream

1½ cups grated Parmesan cheese

2 tablespoons chopped fresh parsley

1 tablespoon chopped fresh tarragon

½ cup sliced almonds

Pour 1 tablespoon of the olive oil into a heavy skillet and set over medium-high heat. Season the chicken breasts with salt and pepper and sear for about 4 minutes on each side, or until golden brown and almost cooked through. Remove the chicken from the skillet and set aside.

Bring a large pot of salted water to a boil and add the linguine. Cook as directed on the package; typically, linguine takes 8 to 10 minutes to cook al dente. Drain the linguine, rinse under running water, and let cool.

Preheat the oven to 350°F. Butter a 2-quart ovenproof casserole dish.

Pour the remaining 1 tablespoon oil into the skillet in which the chicken cooked and set it over medium-high heat. Add the garlic and mushrooms and sauté for 2 or 3 minutes. Add the white wine and deglaze the pan by loosening the solids attached to the bottom with a wooden spoon. Reduce the wine by half, add the velouté, and cook for 2 minutes while stirring. Add the cream and cook for 2 minutes longer. Add the cooked linguine and stir in 1 cup of the Parmesan. Add the parsley and tarragon, season with salt and pepper, and remove from the heat. Transfer the mixture to the prepared casserole. Cut the cooked chicken into thin slices on the bias and place on top of the pasta mixture. Sprinkle the chicken with the remaining Parmesan and the almonds. Bake, uncovered, for 15 minutes.

Remove the casserole from the oven and let rest for 10 minutes before bringing to the table and serving.

CHEF'S NOTES: I was inspired to include this recipe after reading Helen Corbitt's version of chicken Tetrazzini. It makes a great dish for entertaining, as it can be prepared ahead of time and then baked in the oven, leaving you free to attend to your guests. Serve with a big salad.

SERVES: 6 TO 8

SIMPLICITY: + + +

CHICKEN BREAST

Stuffed with Prosciutto, Fontina, and Spinach à la Française

This popular winter dish at Neiman Marcus originated during my days in the kitchen at Cipriani's, the restaurant at the Thunderhead Lodge in Steamboat Springs, Colorado. It became our signature item, and we served at least fifty every night. The clincher for many of our guests was the sublime brown butter—caper sauce, and we were often asked to serve extra on the side. For me, what makes this dish distinctive is the hint of nutmeg in the coating for the chicken.

6 skinless, boneless chicken breasts, about
    6 ounces each

¼ teaspoon grated nutmeg

Salt and freshly ground black pepper to taste

6 thin slices prosciutto, about ⅛-inch thick

6 slices Fontina cheese, about ¼-inch thick

1 cup spinach leaves, lightly packed

2 tablespoons olive oil

4 large eggs

2 cups coarsely grated Parmesan cheese

1 cup all-purpose flour

3 tablespoons unsalted butter

2 tablespoons capers, rinsed and drained

Juice of ½ lemon

2 tablespoons chopped fresh parsley, for garnish

Place the chicken on a cutting board and cover with a piece of plastic wrap. Using a kitchen mallet or a heavy skillet, pound the breasts to an even ½-inch thickness. Remove the plastic wrap and season the chicken with the nutmeg, salt, and pepper. Wrap 1 slice of prosciutto around 1 slice of cheese and place on top of 1 chicken breast. Arrange some of the spinach leaves on top of the prosciutto and then fold the chicken over in half to make a package. Repeat for the other chicken breasts. Chill in the refrigerator for 1 hour.

Preheat the oven to 350°F.

Pour the oil into a nonstick sauté pan and set over medium-low heat. Break the eggs into a bowl and beat lightly; stir in the Parmesan. Place the flour in another bowl. Dip each stuffed chicken breast first in the flour and then in the egg mixture. Transfer 2 of the chicken breasts at a time to the sauté pan and brown on the first side for 1 or 2 minutes. Using a spatula, carefully turn the chicken over and brown on the other

side for 1 or 2 minutes. Transfer the stuffed chicken breasts to a baking sheet and, once all the chicken has been browned, place in the oven and bake for 15 to 20 minutes, or until cooked through.

While the chicken is baking, melt the butter in a small saucepan over medium heat. When the butter begins to brown, add the capers and lemon juice and season with salt and pepper. Keep warm. Remove the chicken from the oven and place on warm serving plates. Pour the caper mixture over the chicken and garnish with the parsley.

CHEF'S NOTE: Serve with pasta dressed lightly with basil oil or basil butter, or a simple green salad.

SERVES: 6

SIMPLICITY: + + + +

CREAMED CHICKEN À LA KING
in a Savory Parmesan Popover

There are almost as many theories about the origins of chicken à la king as there are recipes. Whatever the theory, at least the key ingredients remain the same—chicken, mushrooms, green bell peppers, pimientos, and sherry—but I believe we are the first to introduce popovers into the equation. The earliest stories date from the 1880s, placing the point of origin either in London (Claridge's Hotel) or New York, but there are problems of plausibility. I think the most likely version is that Chef George Greenwald created the dish at the Brighton Beach Hotel in New York around 1900, preparing a special chicken dish one evening for the owners, Mr. and Mrs. E. Clark King II. Mr. King liked it so much that the next day he proposed keeping it on the hotel menu. Chicken à la King, offered at $1.25, quickly became a great success.

2 tablespoons unsalted butter

1 cup sliced button mushrooms

1 large onion, finely sliced

2 large green bell peppers, seeded and finely sliced

¼ cup dry sherry

3 cups warm Velouté (page 278)

3 sprigs fresh tarragon, chopped

2 sprigs fresh thyme, chopped

4 cups diced chicken meat (page 98)

½ cup sliced pimientos

2 tablespoons chopped fresh parsley, plus 6 sprigs for garnish

Salt and freshly ground white pepper to taste

6 Savory Parmesan Popovers (page 27)

Preheat the oven to 350°F.

Melt the butter in a large sauté pan over medium-low heat and add the mushrooms, onion, and bell peppers. Sauté for 3 to 4 minutes, or until softened. Add the sherry and stir for 1 minute. Add the velouté, tarragon, and thyme and bring the mixture to a simmer. Add the chicken and pimientos and cook for 2 minutes. Add the chopped parsley and season with salt and pepper.

Warm the popovers in the oven for 3 minutes and then place them in the center of large soup plates or shallow bowls. With a sharp knife, make a slit in the top of each popover and gently spread it open. Ladle the chicken mixture into the popovers and garnish with the parley sprigs.

CHEF'S NOTES: Serve this dish with rice—the traditional accompaniment—or a flat noodle. When I first started making this recipe, I served it over a homemade biscuit instead of the popover, which was also delicious.

SERVES: 6

SIMPLICITY: + + + +

Part of training as a restaurant chef involves cooking staff meals for kitchen and front-of-house employees, a chore that is typically layered into the day's assignments. In order to complete my other duties in time for dinner service, I often improvised a family-style meal, usually to the distaste of my colleagues. Then I hit upon a last-minute way of making chicken taste really special, and this recipe was favored by everyone. If you are feeling pinched for time, try this tasty roasted chicken; I hope you get the same results I did . . . and still do.

½ cup olive oil

2 teaspoons paprika

2 teaspoons garlic powder

2 teaspoons dried thyme

⅛ teaspoon cayenne pepper

¼ teaspoon crushed fennel seed

1 tablespoon kosher salt

¼ teaspoon freshly ground black pepper

2 chicken breasts, bone in, skin on, about
1¼ pounds each

2 chicken thighs, bone in, skin on

2 chicken legs, bone in, skin on

10 new potatoes, about 1½ pounds, cut in half

½ cup dry white wine

2 tablespoons unsalted butter, diced

Preheat the oven to 375°F.

Place the olive oil in a medium bowl and add the paprika, garlic powder, thyme, cayenne, fennel, salt, and pepper. Mix well and then add the chicken pieces and potatoes, coating them thoroughly on all sides. Transfer the chicken, skin side up, and the potatoes to a large roasting pan. Roast in the oven for 20 minutes; the chicken breasts may be cooked through first, in which case remove them and keep warm. When all the chicken and the potatoes are roasted, set aside and keep warm. Set the roasting pan on the stovetop over medium-low heat and pour in the wine. Deglaze the pan by scraping the solids attached to the bottom with a wooden spoon. Let the wine simmer for 1 minute and then add the butter, stirring until it is melted. Return the chicken pieces to the pan and mix with the sauce. Transfer to warm serving plates and serve with the potatoes.

CHEF'S NOTE: At Neiman Marcus, we serve this dish with a simple green salad.

SERVES: 6

SIMPLICITY: + +

meat and game

STUFFED LAMB RACK
   with Roasted Veggies

CORNED BEEF
   with Braised Cabbage and Boiled Potatoes

"WHY WE LOVE" CORNED BEEF HASH

BEEF AND VEGETABLE KABOBS

TENDERLOIN OF BEEF
   Wrapped with Filo, Lobster, and Boursin

BRAISED VEAL SHANKS

KG'S BIRTHDAY ROASTED SHOULDER OF PORK
   with Roasted Brussels Sprouts

BBQ-GLAZED PORK TENDERLOIN

VENISON CHILI
   with Baked Cheddar Grits

ROAST ELK STEAKS
   with Red Wine Butter and Spaetzle

ONE OF MY defining food memories is my family's Sunday dinner. After a late breakfast when we returned from Mass, the dinner roast went into the oven. We usually skipped lunch, as dinner was served at about 4:30 P.M. All afternoon, the aroma of the dinner roasting pervaded the house, and I just couldn't wait for mealtime. In this chapter, I share some of my own favorite recipes, together with some of Helen Corbitt's that she left for us in her files. When it comes to cooking meat, my favorite technique is slow-cooking—a method to which Helen Corbitt was also partial.

Cooking meat is rewarding not only because of the endless variety of textures and flavors in meat but also because of its nutritional qualities. These factors are often overlooked when stories are written about health concerns related to eating meat. These days, beef and pork are bred much leaner than they used to be, while venison and other free-range game meat are particularly low in cholesterol. Meat contains important minerals, vitamins, and amino acids, and its high protein content is generally regarded as an important element in a healthy diet. As with most things in life, I go along with the dictum of "all things in moderation"; most of these recipes assume portions of 6 ounces or so.

A final word about buying beef and other red meat. Choose cuts that appear moist but not damp, and look for a uniform, bright red color. The most important factor in determining flavor in meat is the degree of marbling, or internal fat. Some people assume that lean meat is more tender, but in fact the opposite is true. As meat cooks, the marbling melts and surrounds the fiber, locking in flavor and aroma. Look for white (not yellow) marbling, and favor cuts that have it running consistently through the meat.

STUFFED LAMB RACK
with Roasted Veggies

This recipe of Helen Corbitt's caught my eye because I had never considered pairing lamb and chicken livers. At first the combination seemed a little strange, but the more I thought about it, the more it intrigued me. I decided to try it out for a cooking class, and I have to say, if those are two ingredients you enjoy, then you will want to make this excellent dish again and again.

7 tablespoons unsalted butter, softened

1 cup chicken livers (about 8 ounces)

6 garlic cloves

1 large shallot, minced

1 cup wild mushrooms, sliced

Salt and coarsely ground black pepper to taste

2 large lamb racks, 12 to 14 ounces each

1 tablespoon Dijon mustard

2 cups prepared unseasoned bread crumbs

½ tablespoon dried rosemary

1 cup Chicken Broth (page 267) or store-bought chicken stock

Roasted Veggies (page 203)

To prepare the lamb, melt 2 tablespoons of the butter in a small skillet over medium heat. Add the chicken livers and sauté for 2 minutes. Add the garlic, shallot, and mushrooms and sauté for 5 minutes longer. Once the livers are no longer red in color, season with salt and pepper, remove from the heat, and transfer the mixture to a bowl. Once it is cool enough to handle, roughly chop the liver mixture and set aside.

Using a sharp knife, butterfly the lamb by cutting down between the bone and the loin meat, leaving about ½ inch of the loin meat still attached to the bone (see photo). Using a kitchen mallet, lightly flatten the lamb loin meat. Rub each loin with 1 tablespoon of the butter. Season with salt and pepper and then spread the liver mixture over the loin meat. Roll up the loin and secure to the bone with long toothpicks, skewers, or butcher's twine. Set the lamb in a roasting pan and rub the outside of each rack with 1 tablespoon of the butter and ½ tablespoon of the mustard. In a bowl, mix the bread crumbs with the rosemary and coat the lamb racks with this mixture. Transfer the lamb to the refrigerator for 1 hour to set up.

Preheat the oven to 375°F.

Roast the lamb for 40 minutes, or until the internal temperature reaches 125°F to 130°F for medium-rare. Remove the lamb from the oven and set aside on a platter. Cool for 10 minutes to allow the juices to settle. Place the roasting pan on the stovetop and set over medium-low heat. Pour in the chicken broth and bring to a simmer. Stir the remaining 1 tablespoon butter into the sauce and let it melt.

To serve, slice the stuffed lamb racks into chops and place 2 or 3 chops on each warm serving plate. Spoon the sauce over the chops and serve with the roasted veggies.

CHEF'S NOTE: Imported lamb racks from Australia or New Zealand, the kind we tested for this recipe, tend to be smaller than domestic ones. If you choose to use domestic racks, increase the roasting time to 45 or 50 minutes but use the same quantities and method given for the other ingredients.

SERVES: 6

SIMPLICITY: + + + + +

CORNED BEEF

with Braised Cabbage and Boiled Potatoes

March 17, St. Patrick's Day, does not go unnoticed in my house, nor did it in Helen Corbitt's kitchen. Being that we are both of Irish descent, this cookbook would not be complete without a great corned beef and cabbage recipe. After reviewing Helen's way of cooking this tribute dish to the patron saint of Ireland (who happens to share the same name as my son), I think I have come up with a good, basic way to make any Irish lad or lassie sing for more supper.

FOR THE CORNED BEEF

2 flat-cut corned beef briskets, about 3 pounds each

1 large head green cabbage, about 2¾ pounds, chopped

2½ pounds Red Bliss potatoes (medium size), halved

1 large onion, cut into large dice

6 garlic cloves

FOR THE HORSERADISH–SOUR CREAM SAUCE

5 teaspoons prepared horseradish

5 tablespoons sour cream

½ teaspoon kosher salt

¼ teaspoon freshly squeezed lemon juice

Dash of Worcestershire sauce

Dash of Tabasco sauce

To prepare the corned beef, place the briskets in a 10-quart Crock-Pot or slow roaster (or a stockpot). If the corned beef brisket comes with a packet of additional pickling spice, add the contents to the pot. Add 2 quarts water or enough to cover the briskets by 2 inches. Bring to a boil, reduce the heat to medium-low, and simmer, covered, for about 1½ hours. Add the cabbage, potatoes, onion, and garlic and simmer for about 1 hour longer, or until the corned beef, cabbage, and potatoes are fork tender and the internal temperature of the corned beef reaches 160°F. If the water level becomes too low during the cooking process, add more to cover the meat and potatoes.

While the corned beef is cooking, prepare the horseradish–sour cream sauce. Place all of the ingredients in a bowl and thoroughly combine; keep refrigerated.

To serve, remove the corned beef and vegetables from the roaster. Carve the brisket and serve with the vegetables and horseradish–sour cream sauce on the side.

CHEF'S NOTES: Allow 35 to 40 minutes per pound for the brisket. Corned beef can never be cooked enough; it should be falling apart and melting in your mouth. A good way to tell if it's cooked is to try breaking the fibers of the meat with a fork. If you can, it's done; if not, keep cooking it. Leftovers can be used for the Corned Beef Hash on page 167.

SERVES: 6 TO 8

SIMPLICITY: + +

This throwback recipe is a tribute to my father-in-law, Bill Ruth, also known affectionately as "the king of hash." Bill was born in New York and then moved his family to Dallas. He enjoyed cooking, and hash was his specialty; he cooked it a lot. He always encouraged his children to finish whatever was on their plates because, as he used to say, "Let's hope there's no leftovers, or guess who'll be eating hash tomorrow!" Make plenty, because it's just as good the next day and even the day after that. Note that you will need to bake and cool the potatoes ahead of time.

FOR THE CORNED BEEF HASH

4 tablespoons (½ stick) unsalted butter

1 onion, finely diced

1 poblano chile, seeded and finely diced

2 Idaho potatoes (about 1½ pounds), baked, cooled, peeled, and grated

1¼ pounds cooked corned beef (page 166), finely diced

1 tablespoon Worcestershire sauce

2 dashes Tabasco sauce

2 large eggs, beaten

Salt and freshly ground black pepper to taste

FOR THE POACHED EGGS

¼ cup white vinegar

12 large eggs, at room temperature

To prepare the hash, melt 2 tablespoons of the butter in a large nonstick skillet over medium heat. Add the onion and poblano and sauté for 2 minutes. Remove from the heat and let cool. Transfer to a bowl and add the grated potatoes, corned beef, Worcestershire sauce, Tabasco, and eggs. Season with salt and pepper and mix thoroughly. Transfer to the refrigerator and let sit for 2 to 3 hours so the flavors can marry.

Melt the remaining 2 tablespoons butter in a large skillet and add the hash mixture. Cook over medium-low heat for 8 to 10 minutes, until golden and crispy, stirring occasionally with a spatula so the hash browns evenly.

While the hash is cooking, prepare the poached eggs. Pour 2 quarts water into a saucepan, salt lightly, and add the vinegar. Bring almost to a simmer (180°F to 190°F) and then gently crack the eggs into the water, as close to the surface as possible. Cook the eggs in 3 or 4 batches for 3½ to 4 minutes (depending on desired doneness). Remove with a slotted spoon, allowing excess water to drain, and gently blot dry with paper towels.

Spoon the hash onto serving plates and top each serving with 2 poached eggs.

CHEF'S NOTES: Grate the baked potato on a large-hole grater. Feel free to substitute fried eggs, scrambled eggs, or any other style of eggs for the poached eggs.

SERVES: 6

SIMPLICITY: + +

BEEF AND VEGETABLE KABOBS

Back in the day, when Helen Corbitt was making a big impression at Neiman Marcus, kabobs were cutting-edge and distinctly exotic. Not only were they from far-off, seldom-traveled lands but also they were grilled, long before that technique was embraced by a hungry nation. Kabobs have remained a timeless classic because of their festive, colorful qualities, their subtle flavors, and their simplicity. Notice that in this recipe of Helen's, we grill the vegetables and the meat on different skewers. The most common problem with home-cooked kabobs is that the vegetables begin to singe while the meat is still rare. This way, like ingredients get cooked for the same amount of time and so come off the grill just right.

½ cup olive oil

¼ cup honey

2 tablespoons white wine vinegar

2 tablespoons soy sauce

2 large garlic cloves, minced

2 tablespoons minced fresh parsley

1 teaspoon ground ginger

2½ pounds beef sirloin, cut into 1½-inch cubes

Salt and coarsely ground black pepper to taste

2 large onions, cut into 1½-inch cubes

2 large green bell peppers, seeded and cut into
   1½-inch squares

12 button mushrooms, stemmed

12 canned or bottled artichoke hearts, cut in half

12 cherry tomatoes

Combine the oil and honey in a large bowl and add the vinegar, soy sauce, garlic, parsley, and ginger. Mix together thoroughly. Season the beef with salt and pepper and add to the marinade. Cover and marinate in the refrigerator for 2 hours.

Soak 18 bamboo skewers in water for 20 minutes.

Prepare the grill.

Thread the beef, onions, and bell peppers together on 12 of the skewers. Thread the mushrooms, artichokes, and tomatoes on the remaining 6 skewers. Brush all the skewers with the marinade. Set the skewers on the grill over medium heat and grill for 10 to 12 minutes, turning the skewers 2 or 3 times. Serve with rice, the Wild Mushroom Risotto (page 210), or Oven-Fried Potatoes (page 208).

CHEF'S NOTE: After putting the skewers on the grill and brushing with the marinade, do not brush the kabobs further, as the marinade is not cooked.

SERVES: 6

SIMPLICITY: + +

TENDERLOIN OF BEEF
Wrapped with Filo, Lobster, and Boursin

This elegant surf-and-turf combination makes an impressive dish whenever you are entertaining. I like to call it "the company standby" because it never fails to make a memorable impact on guests, who are impressed with both its appearance and taste. In addition, it turns out reliably and can be prepared ahead of time, important qualities when your food is in the spotlight. It is worth mentioning that like any good company recipe, practice makes perfect; be sure to make this one a few times before calling it a house favorite.

6 beef tenderloin filets (filet mignon), about 6 ounces each

Salt and freshly ground white pepper to taste

1½ tablespoons olive oil

4 tablespoons (½ stick) unsalted butter

1 teaspoon minced garlic

1 cup sliced cremini mushrooms

2 cups spinach leaves

2 tablespoons Boursin cheese

1 pound cooked lobster meat (page 130), diced

6 sheets filo dough

Preheat the oven to 375°F.

Season the beef filets with salt and pepper. Pour the oil into a cast-iron skillet and set over medium-high heat. When the oil is hot, add the filets and sear for 2 to 3 minutes on each side, until well browned. Remove the filets from the pan and set aside on a platter to cool. Add 1 tablespoon of the butter to the skillet, add the garlic and mushrooms, and sauté over medium-high heat for 2 minutes, or until softened. Turn off the heat and add the spinach, Boursin, and lobster meat. Season with salt and pepper, mix thoroughly, and let the mixture cool.

In a small saucepan (or in the microwave), melt the remaining 3 tablespoons butter. Lay out the filo sheets on a clean work surface and cover completely with a damp kitchen towel. Working with 1 sheet of filo at a time, remove from beneath the towel and place on a clean work surface. Brush with the melted butter and fold the filo sheet in half. Brush with butter again and fold in half again

lengthwise. Once more, brush the top of the filo with butter. Place a beef filet on the work surface and wrap with the filo, forming a cylinder around the filet with a 1-inch lip of filo extending above the meat on all sides (see the photo on page 172). Brush the outside of the filo with butter and fill the cylinder (on top of the filet) with the lobster and Boursin mixture. Repeat for the remaining filo and filets.

Transfer the wrapped beef to a roasting pan and bake in the oven for 30 minutes. If the filo tops seem to be browning too early, place a piece of foil over them and keep covered until the meat is fully cooked. Remove from the oven and let the filets rest for 2 minutes before serving.

CHEF'S NOTE: I like to serve this dish with Scalloped Potatoes (page 204), another elegant presentation.

SERVES: 6

SIMPLICITY: + + + +

BRAISED VEAL SHANKS

Here is my version of the Italian classic dish from the Piedmont region, osso buco. Slow cooking, and particularly braising, is my favorite method because the flavor builds from the meat's natural juices as it becomes progressively tender with time. In this case, the deep, rich, and complex flavors of the shanks belie their rather plain appearance. Lamb shanks and beef short ribs can also be cooked this way.

3 tablespoons olive oil

6 veal shanks, preferably center cut, 12 ounces to
   1 pound each

Salt and freshly ground black pepper to taste

¼ cup all-purpose flour, for dredging

1 large onion, diced

2 carrots, peeled and diced

2 celery stalks, diced

3 garlic cloves

6 sprigs fresh thyme

2 dried bay leaves

1 teaspoon black peppercorns

2 tablespoons tomato paste

1½ cups dry red wine

4 cups Beef Broth (page 268) or store-bought
   beef stock

Preheat the oven to 300°F.

Pour 2 tablespoons of the olive oil into a large ovenproof saucepan and set over medium heat. Season the veal shanks on all sides with salt and pepper and dredge lightly in the flour. Add the veal shanks to the hot oil and sear for 2 to 3 minutes on each side, until lightly browned. Set the shanks aside on a platter. Add the remaining 1 tablespoon oil to the saucepan and add the onion, carrots, celery, and garlic. Sauté for 5 minutes, scraping the solids off the bottom of the pan with a wooden spoon. Add the thyme, bay leaves, and peppercorns and continue cooking for 5 or 6 minutes longer, until the vegetables begin to caramelize. Add the tomato paste and cook for 1 minute. Add the red wine and deglaze the pan, stirring again with a wooden spoon to dislodge any solids attached to the bottom of the pan. Reduce the wine by two-thirds and then add the beef broth. Stir well and return the veal shanks to the pan, making sure there is enough broth to completely cover the veal; add a little more if necessary. Bring to a simmer and cook for 5 minutes. Cover the pan with a lid and transfer to the oven for 3 hours, or until the veal is fork tender.

After the veal is cooked, remove the shanks from the pan with a slotted spoon and keep warm. Place the pan on the stovetop and bring the sauce to a simmer. Reduce by half over medium heat, 20 to 25 minutes, skimming any fat that rises to the surface. Strain the sauce through a fine sieve, discarding the solids. Return the veal shanks to the sauce and continue to reduce for about 5 minutes longer.

To serve, place a veal shank in each serving bowl. Spoon some of the sauce over the veal and serve with risotto (page 210) or mashed potatoes.

CHEF'S NOTES: Use an ovenproof, deep-sided, 8-quart saucepan or cast-iron Dutch oven with a lid for this recipe. Consider serving some nice roasted root vegetables with this dish.

SERVES: 6

SIMPLICITY: + + + +

KG'S BIRTHDAY ROASTED SHOULDER OF PORK
with Roasted Brussels Sprouts

When I was growing up, one of the special things about celebrating our birthdays was that my mom let us pick our favorite meal and then she would prepare it for dinner. From the earliest birthdays I can remember, this dish is what I asked for. It's special to me for another reason. My mom tells me it was made for her by my grandmother the day before I was born. Perhaps that's why I like it so much—I just had to put in an appearance in the world to get some more! I have to admit I no longer have to wait for my birthday to enjoy this great recipe. Most any Sunday would work well at our house!

FOR THE PORK

6 pounds pork shoulder

2 tablespoons kosher salt

1 tablespoon coarsely ground black pepper

2 tablespoons Dijon mustard

1 onion, thinly sliced

3 carrots, peeled and chopped

3 turnips, peeled and chopped

4 garlic cloves

FOR THE ROASTED BRUSSELS SPROUTS

1½ pounds Brussels sprouts (about 30 sprouts), trimmed

2½ tablespoons extra-virgin olive oil

Salt and freshly ground black pepper to taste

FOR THE GRAVY

4 cups Chicken Broth (page 267) or store-bought chicken stock

2 chicken bouillon cubes

½ cup all-purpose flour

Preheat the oven to 375°F.

To prepare the pork, place the pork shoulder in a large roasting pan, fat side up, and season with the salt and pepper. Brush the mustard over the pork and top with half of the sliced onion. Surround the pork with the remaining onion, the carrots, turnips, and garlic. Transfer to the oven and roast for 1 hour. Reduce the oven temperature to 350°F, cover the roast with foil, and continue roasting for 1 hour longer. Uncover the roast and continue cooking for 45 minutes, or until the internal temperature of the pork reaches 180°F.

While the pork is roasting, prepare the sprouts. Place the sprouts in a bowl, sprinkle with the oil, and season with salt and pepper. Toss together and then spread out the sprouts in a large roasting pan. Transfer to the oven and roast for 30 minutes, or until lightly browned, stirring occasionally.

To make the gravy, remove the roast from the pan and set aside on a platter to rest. Put the roasting pan on the stovetop and turn the heat to low; skim off as much of the fat from the pan juices as possible and discard. Remove the turnips and the carrots and place with the roast pork on the platter. Scrape the bottom of the pan with a wooden spoon, pour in the chicken broth and the bouillon cubes and bring to a simmer. Reduce the broth by one-quarter. In a small cup, mix the flour with ½ cup water and stir with a fork, eliminating any lumps. Add the flour mixture bit by bit to the simmering broth, until the gravy reaches the desired thickness.

To serve, slice the pork and arrange on warm serving plates. Spoon the roasted sprouts next to the pork and pour the gravy over.

CHEF'S NOTES: The slow roasting process caramelizes the vegetables to perfection. The gravy is so good you might want to consider doubling the recipe to enjoy with the leftovers the next day. I find that store-bought chicken stock works particularly well in this recipe.

SERVES: 6 TO 8

SIMPLICITY: + + +

BBQ-GLAZED PORK TENDERLOIN

Pork tenderloin is an underrated cut of meat that is used all too rarely, especially in higher-end restaurants. This is a shame because it has great flavor and tenderness, if cooked properly, and it is easy to prepare. Some people associate pork with fattier cuts, but pork is bred much leaner than it used to be. This recipe is a particular family favorite; we enjoy it at home at least twice a month. I recommend the Stuffed Twice-Baked Potatoes (page 207) and/or the Spring Salad Kilkenny (page 111) as ideal accompaniments.

3 pounds pork tenderloin, trimmed of fat

2 tablespoons barbecue spice

1 large onion, sliced

6 garlic cloves, sliced

2 cups Neiman Marcus BBQ Sauce (page 271)

Salt and coarsely ground black pepper to taste

Place the pork tenderloins in a shallow dish and rub with the barbecue spice. Scatter the sliced onion and garlic around and over the pork and cover with 1 cup of the BBQ sauce. Cover the dish with plastic wrap and marinate the pork in the refrigerator for 4 to 6 hours.

Prepare the grill.

Remove the pork from the marinade (discard the marinade) and season with salt and pepper. Cook the pork over medium heat, initially rotating it frequently to brown on all sides, about 10 minutes. Brush the tenderloins with some of the additional 1 cup BBQ sauce and close the lid of the grill. After another 5 minutes, turn the pork over and brush with the sauce. Continue this process every 5 minutes, until the pork is cooked through and reaches an internal temperature of 165°F, 25 to 30 minutes of total cooking time. Let the tenderloins rest for 5 minutes before slicing and serving.

CHEF'S NOTES: I prefer Head Country barbecue spice, made in Oklahoma, but any good-quality barbecue seasoning will work fine. It is important to grill the pork over medium heat; any higher, and you risk scorching and burning the pork before it is cooked through.

SERVES: 6 TO 8

SIMPLICITY: + +

VENISON CHILI
with Baked Cheddar Grits

Living in Texas and being a chef, I am often treated to friends dropping by during hunting season with venison in hopes it might earn them an invitation for dinner—and they're usually in luck. Typically, hunters know what to do with the loins and saddles; it is the tougher cuts such as the shoulder and legs that get left behind. Chili is the ideal answer. The grits round out a true Old West experience.

2 large dried ancho chiles, stemmed

5 pounds diced venison stew meat from the shoulder and/or leg

Salt and coarsely ground black pepper to taste

½ cup olive oil

1 large onion, finely diced

1 large poblano chile, finely diced

1 jalapeño, seeded and minced

3 garlic cloves, crushed

2 tablespoons pure chili powder

3 tablespoons all-purpose flour

1 cup canned diced tomatoes with their juice

¾ cup dark beer

3 cups Beef Broth (page 268) or store-bought beef stock

1 cup cooked black beans

1 cup cooked corn kernels

2 tablespoons chopped fresh cilantro

2 tablespoons honey

Juice of 1 lime

Baked Cheddar Grits (page 209)

Place the anchos in a small saucepan with 1 cup water and bring to a boil. Simmer for 2 minutes, or until the chiles are softened. Transfer ⅓ cup of the liquid and the chiles to a blender and purée to a smooth paste; reserve.

Season the stew meat generously with the salt and pepper. Pour 2 tablespoons of the oil into a large saucepan and set over medium-high heat. When the oil is hot, add one-quarter of the venison and brown the meat on all sides. Remove the venison with a slotted spoon and set aside on a platter. Repeat the process, cooking the meat in batches. When all the meat has been browned, using the oil left in the pan, add the onion, poblano, jalapeño, and garlic. Sauté for 4 minutes, return the meat to the pan, and season with the chili powder. Sprinkle the flour over the meat and use a wooden spoon to make sure it is well coated. Stir in the tomatoes and the reserved ancho chile paste. Pour in the beer and the beef broth and bring to a simmer. Reduce the heat to low, cover

the pan, and cook the stew for 1 hour. Check the meat for doneness by removing a piece and slicing it with a knife; the knife should slice through the meat easily. Fold in the beans, corn, cilantro, honey, and lime juice. Adjust the seasoning with salt and pepper. To serve, ladle the chili into warm serving bowls and serve with the grits.

CHEF'S NOTE: Ancho chiles are dried poblano chiles. They are deep, dark red in color and have mildly hot, sweet, and flavorful tones. Buy anchos that are soft and supple; if they seem dry and brittle, they are old and stale.

SERVES: 6 TO 8

SIMPLICITY: + + +

ROASTED ELK STEAKS
with Red Wine Butter and Spaetzle

Elk is a healthful meat, as it is low in cholesterol and has a lower fat content than other red meats, poultry, and even most fish. Like venison, elk is now being raised commercially in free-range conditions, under USDA regulations. It also has the advantage of not being treated with hormones or antibiotics. Of course, in the Midwest and the western United States it is a favorite hunting quarry, and I created this recipe after a friend dropped off some steaks from an elk he had harvested in the Rocky Mountains. The secret to this recipe is the lengthy marinating time, which allows the flavors to come together.

6 to 8 elk or venison filets, about 6 ounces each

4 garlic cloves, crushed

1½ tablespoons kosher salt

1½ tablespoons coarsely ground black pepper

1 onion, thinly sliced

4 sprigs fresh thyme

1 tablespoon Worcestershire sauce

½ teaspoon Tabasco sauce

1¼ cups dry red wine

2 tablespoons olive oil

6 to 8 slices apple-smoked or sugar-cured bacon

3 tablespoons unsalted butter

Spaetzle (page 213)

To prepare the steaks, rub the filets with the garlic and season with salt and pepper. Transfer the steaks and garlic to a casserole dish and add the onion, thyme, Worcestershire sauce, and Tabasco. Mix together and then pour in 1 cup of the wine. Cover and let marinate in the refrigerator for 6 to 8 hours.

Preheat the oven to 375°F.

Pour the olive oil into a large cast-iron or other ovenproof skillet and set over medium-high heat. Remove the filets from the marinade and pat dry. Wrap each fillet with a slice of bacon and secure with a toothpick. Season the steaks with salt and pepper and add to the skillet. Sauté for 3 or 4 minutes on each side, or until well browned. Transfer the skillet to the oven and roast the filets for about 25 minutes for medium-rare, or until the internal temperature reaches 125°F to 130°F.

Remove the filets to a serving platter and place the skillet on the stovetop over medium-low heat. Pour in the remaining ¼ cup wine and deglaze the pan by scraping the bottom with a wooden spoon to dislodge the solids. Reduce the wine by half and then add the butter. When the mixture begins to foam, return the filets to the pan and coat them with the sauce.

To serve, transfer the filets to warm serving plates. Spoon the sauce from the skillet next to the filets and serve with the spaetzle.

CHEF'S NOTES: For notes on the traditional German dish of spaetzle, see page 213. Wrapping the elk with the bacon is a great way to add flavor to the lean elk steaks, which, unlike typical cuts of beef, do not have much marbling. By all means leave the bacon out if you prefer.

SERVES: 6 TO 8

SIMPLICITY: + + +

side dishes

SWEET POTATO PONE

NEW ENGLAND CABBAGE SALAD

POTATO LATKES

COLESLAW

SPINACH SOUFFLÉ

CARROT SOUFFLÉ

EGGPLANT PARMESAN

SWEET SUMMER CORN PUDDING

BRAISED BELGIAN ENDIVE

ROASTED VEGGIES

SCALLOPED POTATOES

STUFFED TWICE-BAKED POTATOES

OVEN-FRIED POTATOES

BAKED CHEDDAR GRITS

WILD MUSHROOM RISOTTO

PINE NUT–STUDDED WILD RICE

SPAETZLE

AS A YOUNG CHEF, I became so enamored of vegetable dishes that for a brief period I became a vegetarian, eschewing all meat. Though I have once again an omnivorous diet, I still appreciate the role sides can play. The recipes in this chapter are a combination of delicious personal favorites; some are Helen Corbitt's (or adaptations thereof) and others are mine. I guarantee these side dishes will dress up your meal and make many people happy around your dining table. I love the idea of side dishes, and it is hard for me to understand the reluctance of some cooks to give them the prominence they merit. Side dishes take me back to some of the meals we kids shared with our neighbors. Many times it worked out that my family would go over to the Gottliebs or the Ponentes, bringing a side dish to complement whatever they had made. Mom might make her wonderful scalloped potato dish and garnish it with a generous sprinkling of paprika and parsley, and that, along with a fresh-baked cake, would be our family's contribution to a memorable multifamily meal.

Side dishes come into their own when you're invited to a potluck supper, and these recipes will certainly impress. Thanksgiving would not be Thanksgiving without side dishes. I remember holiday gatherings for the numerous casserole dishes presented on the buffet in my grandmom's dining room and loving every little spoonful on my plate. I can still hear the grownups' admonition ringing in my ears: "Now be sure you finish everything you put on your plate," and on those rare occasions when I didn't finish everything, "See? Your eyes are bigger than your stomach!" Happy days.

SWEET POTATO PONE

Mark Twain famously wrote, "You tell me whar a man gits his corn pone, en I'll tell you what his 'pinions is." Pone (sometimes called **Indian pone***) originated in the northern part of the country but soon became a Southern favorite that usually took the form of a soft corn bread; as this recipe proves, it can also be made with sweet potatoes. If you add a little more sugar, you could also serve it as a dessert, which is how it is enjoyed in many parts of the Midwest as well as the South. I like to make this recipe during the holiday season with turkey dinner, ham, or prime rib; it is also delicious served cold.*

---

4 large sweet potatoes, peeled

5 large eggs

2 cans (14 ounces each) sweetened condensed
　milk

1 teaspoon vanilla extract

½ cup milk

2 tablespoons unsalted butter, plus additional for
　the baking dish

1 teaspoon ground cinnamon

1 cup chopped pecans

Preheat the oven to 350°F. Generously butter an 11-inch round ceramic or glass baking dish.

Grate the sweet potatoes directly into a bowl using the fine side of the grater; there should be about 6 cups grated sweet potato. In a separate bowl, whisk the eggs with the condensed milk, vanilla, and milk. Add the 2 tablespoons butter, cinnamon, and pecans and then add the sweet potatoes. Pour the pone mixture into the prepared baking dish. Transfer to the oven and bake for about 1 hour, or until a toothpick inserted in the center comes out clean.

SERVES: 6 TO 8

SIMPLICITY: + +

NEW ENGLAND CABBAGE SALAD

This simple and flavorful cabbage salad is another of Helen Corbitt's creations; we have altered it only slightly from its original format. It makes a great side, and we pair it at our restaurants with the BBQ Sea Scallops on page 124. I like the idea of a warm marinade that lightly wilts the cabbage and gives it a tantalizing pickled quality.

1 cup white wine vinegar

1 cup sugar

1 teaspoon celery seed

½ teaspoon ground turmeric

1 teaspoon mustard seeds

1 large head green cabbage

1 large green bell pepper, seeded and finely diced

1 onion, finely diced

1 tablespoon olive oil

Salt and freshly ground white pepper to taste

Place the vinegar, sugar, celery seed, turmeric, and mustard seeds in a small saucepan and bring to a simmer. Stir to make sure the sugar is dissolved and then turn off the heat. Using the largest holes of a grater, grate the cabbage into a stainless-steel bowl (there should be 6 to 7 heaping cups grated cabbage). Add the bell pepper and onion and mix well. Pour the hot vinegar mixture over the vegetables and combine thoroughly. Cover the bowl and chill in the refrigerator for 2 hours or, preferably, overnight to allow the flavors to marry. Just before serving, add the olive oil and toss to combine. Season with salt and pepper.

SERVES: 6

SIMPLICITY: + +

POTATO LATKES

Latkes are traditionally enjoyed at Hanukkah, but I am all for giving them a much broader stage at any time of year. I tell anyone willing to listen that Anita Hirsch, our corporate chef at Neiman Marcus, is the queen of latkes. Whenever she makes them, it seems as though she is up to her elbows in potatoes—I guess she just likes to feed people. These latkes are excellent with fried chicken or Friday Night Foil-Roasted Salmon (page 127), or on their own with applesauce.

2 pounds russet potatoes, washed well

1 small onion

2 large eggs, beaten

3 tablespoons minced fresh chives or scallions

Salt and freshly ground white pepper to taste

3 tablespoons olive oil

3 tablespoons sour cream

Preheat the oven to 300°F.

Using a large-hole grater, grate the potatoes and onion directly into a large bowl. Add the eggs and chives and season generously with salt and pepper. Let the mixture sit for about 30 minutes to allow the flavors to marry. As the mixture will have started to weep moisture, mix the ingredients together again.

Pour the olive oil into a large, heavy skillet and set over medium-low heat. Use your fingers to form the potato mixture into 18 to 24 small patties, 2 or 3 inches across, gently squeezing the excess moisture from the potatoes. Cooking the patties in batches, place in the hot skillet and sauté on the first side for 4 or 5 minutes, or until browned. Flip over carefully, using a spatula, and sauté the second side for 5 or 6 minutes. Remove the patties with the spatula and drain on paper towels (it is important to taste a cooked latke from the first batch to check the seasonings; adjust them as necessary). After you have cooked all the latkes, transfer them to a baking sheet and warm in the oven for 10 to 15 minutes. Remove from the oven, transfer to serving plates, and serve with a dollop of sour cream.

SERVES: 6 TO 8

SIMPLICITY: + + + +

COLESLAW

This ever-popular side dish is American in origin, dating from the late nineteenth century, but its name is derived from the Dutch kool sla, *meaning "cabbage salad." Back then it was probably served hot, but the secret to this slaw recipe is to serve it well chilled for best crunch and flavor. We have paired it with crispy chicken (page 143), and it makes the perfect partner for any summer barbecue or picnic.*

1 large head green cabbage

2 scallions, minced

6 sprigs fresh parsley, minced

2 cups mayonnaise

2 tablespoons cider vinegar

2 teaspoons light brown sugar

2 teaspoons prepared horseradish

2 teaspoons granulated sugar

1 teaspoon Worcestershire sauce

½ teaspoon celery salt

½ teaspoon garlic powder

½ teaspoon onion powder

½ teaspoon dry English mustard, such as
   Colman's

¼ teaspoon Tabasco sauce

Salt and freshly ground white pepper to taste

Using the largest holes of a grater, grate the cabbage into a bowl (there should be 6 or 7 heaping cups grated cabbage). In a separate stainless-steel bowl, combine all of the remaining ingredients, using a wire whisk. Fold in the grated cabbage. Cover the bowl and chill in the refrigerator for at least 2 hours before serving.

CHEF'S NOTE: To add a little color, grate a carrot into the mixture.

SERVES: 6

SIMPLICITY: + +

SPINACH SOUFFLÉ

Helen Corbitt loved serving vegetable soufflés; this recipe and the carrot soufflé (page 194) were popular items in the 1950s and '60s. The good news is they are back in fashion. They make elegant buffet items, especially when served together; the color contrast really works.

7 tablespoons unsalted butter, plus additional for
the baking dish

1 shallot, minced

5 cups chopped fresh spinach leaves

7 tablespoons all-purpose flour

2½ cups warm milk

10 large eggs, separated

⅛ teaspoon grated nutmeg

Salt and freshly ground white pepper to taste

Dash of Tabasco sauce

Preheat the oven to 375°F. Butter a 9-inch casserole dish.

Melt the butter in a large, heavy skillet over medium-low heat. Add the shallot and spinach and sauté for 3 minutes. Reduce the heat to low, add the flour, and stir with a wooden spoon to form a roux. Using a wire whisk, slowly whisk in the warm milk until the mixture becomes quite thick. Continue to cook for 3 or 4 minutes longer and then remove from the heat. Transfer to a stainless-steel bowl and let cool.

In a separate bowl, whisk the egg yolks until pale in color. In another bowl, whisk the egg whites until stiff peaks form. Using a spatula, gently fold the egg yolks into the cooled milk mixture and then fold in the egg whites. Stir in the nutmeg, salt, pepper, and Tabasco. Fold the soufflé mixture into the prepared casserole, spreading it out evenly with the spatula. Transfer to the oven and bake for 30 minutes, or until a toothpick inserted in the center comes out clean.

SERVES: 8

SIMPLICITY: + + +

CARROT SOUFFLÉ

As with Helen Corbitt's spinach soufflé (page 191), I didn't need to change a thing in this recipe; when I tested it, the flavors and consistency were impossible to improve upon. If you feel nervous about making soufflés, don't worry—these soufflés won't fall. Serve either soufflé with any red meat—the beef tenderloin wrapped in filo (page 170) makes a fine pairing, for example. This soufflé will also perfectly embellish the "Family Meal" Roast Chicken (page 156) or KG's Birthday Roasted Shoulder of Pork (page 177).

3 carrots, peeled and cut into large dice (about 3 cups)

3 tablespoons cornstarch

1 tablespoon unsalted butter, melted, plus additional for the baking dish

3 large eggs, beaten

2½ cups sweetened condensed milk

1¼ cups heavy cream

1½ teaspoons kosher salt

¼ teaspoon grated nutmeg

Preheat the oven to 325°F. Butter a 9-inch casserole dish.

Bring a saucepan of salted water to a boil, add the carrots, and cook for 20 minutes, or until soft. Drain the carrots, transfer to a food processor, and purée until very smooth. Place the carrot purée in a bowl and add the cornstarch and butter. In a separate bowl, combine the eggs, condensed milk, cream, salt, and nutmeg and whisk together.

Add this mixture to the carrots and stir to thoroughly combine. Transfer the mixture to the prepared casserole, spreading out evenly with a spatula. Transfer to the oven and bake for about 1½ hours, or until a toothpick inserted in the center comes out clean.

SERVES: 8

SIMPLICITY: + +

EGGPLANT PARMESAN

I remember this side dish from my earliest expeditions to restaurants with my parents. Back then, it seemed wildly exotic, and it has remained a firm personal favorite ever since. Its melting quality and down-home nature make it a real comfort food—just the thing to relax with after a hard day's work.

4 eggplants, peeled and cut lengthwise into
   ½-inch-thick slices

2 tablespoons kosher salt

2 cups all-purpose flour

4 cups unseasoned dry bread crumbs

5 large eggs

½ cup olive oil

4 to 5 cups Tomato Sauce (page 270)

2 cups grated Parmesan cheese

8 fresh basil leaves, torn

2 tablespoons minced fresh oregano

3 tablespoons minced fresh parsley

2 pounds mozzarella cheese, cut into ¼-inch slices

Preheat the oven to 350°F.

Place the eggplant slices on a large baking sheet and sprinkle on both sides with a generous pinch of the salt. Let the eggplant sit at room temperature for about 15 minutes.

Place the flour and bread crumbs on separate plates. Beat the eggs in a shallow bowl. Dip an eggplant slice first in the flour, then in the egg wash, and then in the bread crumbs. Transfer to a platter and repeat for the remaining eggplant slices. Heat 2 tablespoons of the olive oil in a large, heavy skillet over medium heat. When the oil is hot, add one-quarter of the eggplant slices and sauté for 2 to 3 minutes on each side, until golden and crisp. Drain the fried eggplant on paper towels while you fry 3 additional batches of eggplant, using the remaining oil.

Ladle 2 cups of the tomato sauce into a 4-quart casserole dish. Arrange a single layer of the cooked eggplant over the sauce and sprinkle with the Parmesan cheese. Add 1 more cup of the tomato sauce and half of the basil leaves, oregano, and parsley. Add a layer of the mozzarella and then repeat the process, beginning with more tomato sauce. Depending on the size of the casserole, if there are enough ingredients, add another layer. Place the casserole dish on a baking sheet, cover with foil, and bake for 30 minutes. Uncover the casserole and bake for 30 minutes longer, or until the internal temperature reaches 165°F.

CHEF'S NOTE: Salting the eggplant and letting it stand draws out its moisture, making the fried slices crisper.

SERVES: 6 TO 8

SIMPLICITY: + + + + +

SWEET SUMMER CORN PUDDING

I have been serving this tasty accompaniment since I created it years ago as a garnish for a large banquet. I had no idea back then how popular it would prove to be. It is certainly versatile—you can just as easily serve the pudding as an appetizer. It is the ideal way to use up plentiful summer corn.

4 ears fresh corn

2 cups half-and-half

3 sprigs fresh thyme

1 tablespoon unsalted butter, plus additional for the ramekins

6 large eggs

2 cups milk

1 teaspoon kosher salt

⅛ teaspoon freshly ground white pepper

1 tablespoon chopped fresh chives

Preheat the oven to 325°F. Lightly butter six to eight 6-ounce ramekins.

Remove the husks and silks from the corn cobs and stand 1 ear on its end on a work surface. Using a sharp knife, carefully cut the kernels from the cob and transfer to a bowl; reserve the cob. Repeat for the remaining corn; you should have about 3 cups kernels. Place all but 1 cup of the corn kernels in a saucepan wide enough to hold the reserved cobs (break the cobs in half if necessary) and add the cobs. Add the half-and-half and the thyme and bring to a simmer; continue to cook at a low simmer for 20 minutes. Remove the cobs and thyme from the pan and discard. Transfer the corn mixture in batches to a blender and purée until smooth (if the mixture is too thick to blend properly, add a little milk). Strain the purée into a bowl using a coarse strainer, pushing down on the puréed corn with a wooden spoon. Let the blended corn mixture cool for 20 minutes.

Melt the butter in a small skillet over medium heat. Add the remaining 1 cup corn kernels and sauté for 4 to 5 min-utes. Remove from the heat and let cool slightly. In a large bowl, whisk the eggs with the milk and add the salt, pepper, the blended corn mixture, sautéed corn, and chives. Whisk well to combine thoroughly. Pour the mixture into the prepared ramekins and place in a water bath (there should be enough water to come halfway up the sides of the ramekins). Cover the ramekins with foil and transfer to the oven. Bake the corn puddings for 1 hour, or until they are set and a toothpick inserted in the center comes out clean.

CHEF'S NOTES: If you prefer the corn puddings to have a little color—a golden brown tinge—do not cover the ramekins with foil. You can unmold the puddings after baking if you wish by letting them cool slightly and running a small knife around the inside edge of the ramekins to loosen. Gently flip the ramekins to release the puddings onto a serving platter.

SERVES: 6

SIMPLICITY: + + + +

BRAISED BELGIAN ENDIVE

I had never set eyes on Belgian endive before I cooked it for the first time as a culinary student. Cigar-shaped and pale green to cream-colored, this member of the chicory family has a bitter flavor, so adding sugar and the other ingredients in this recipe creates a delicious and intriguing balance. I love serving braised endive with roasted beef tenderloin or prime rib.

2 tablespoons unsalted butter

6 heads Belgian endive, cut in half lengthwise

2 tablespoons light brown sugar

½ cup Chicken Broth (page 267) or store-bought
    chicken stock

3 tablespoons balsamic vinegar

Salt and freshly ground white pepper to taste

Preheat the oven to 325°F.

Melt the butter in a large, ovenproof skillet over medium heat. Place the endive in the skillet, cut side down, and brown for 2 or 3 minutes. Using tongs, turn the endive over and brown the other side for 2 minutes. Add the sugar to the pan and coat the endive. Add the broth to the skillet and reduce by half over medium heat, about 3 minutes. Add the vinegar and simmer for 2 min-utes longer. Turn each endive cut side down and bake in the oven for 12 min-utes, or until the endive is fork-tender. Remove from the oven, check the sea-soning for salt and pepper, and set 2 halves of endive on each serving plate.

SERVES: 6

SIMPLICITY: + +

ROASTED VEGGIES

Roasting vegetables doesn't get much simpler than in this great last-minute recipe. Most vegetables lend themselves to roasting, and everyone seems to like them cooked this way. Serve them with any roasted meat or fish. Alternatively, let them cool, sprinkle with balsamic vinegar, and serve chilled with toast points as an antipasto.

1 eggplant, unpeeled, cut crosswise into ¾-inch slices

1 large yellow squash, cut on the bias into ½-inch slices

1 large zucchini, cut on the bias into ½-inch slices

¼ cup olive oil

Salt and coarsely ground black pepper to taste

1 tablespoon minced garlic

1 tablespoon fresh thyme leaves

2 sprigs fresh rosemary

Preheat the oven to 400°F.

Place the eggplant, squash, and zucchini in a bowl, add the olive oil, and toss well to coat the vegetables thoroughly. Arrange the veggies in a single layer on a baking sheet and season with salt and pepper. Scatter the garlic, thyme, and rosemary over the veggies and transfer to the oven. Roast for about 30 minutes, or until the veggies start to brown. Remove from the oven. To serve, arrange the squash and zucchini on top of the eggplant slices.

SERVES: 6 TO 8

SIMPLICITY: +

SCALLOPED POTATOES

This creamy layered potato dish will fill your kitchen with the aromas of nutmeg and garlic. That alone is almost enough to fill you up! Sometimes it's hard to be patient when this elegant classic comes out of the oven bubbly and hot, but it's important to let it settle for a few minutes before spooning it out so the potatoes can firm up a bit.

2 garlic cloves, crushed

2 pounds russet potatoes, peeled and cut into
   ¼-inch slices

1 teaspoon grated nutmeg

Salt and freshly ground white pepper to taste

2 cups half-and-half

1 cup heavy cream

Preheat the oven to 350°F. Butter a 5 by 7-inch casserole dish and rub with the crushed garlic.

Place the sliced potatoes in a large saucepan filled with cold water; drain the potatoes and arrange a layer on the bottom of the prepared casserole. Add a second layer on top and season with a dash of nutmeg and a little salt and pepper. Continue layering the potatoes in the casserole, seasoning alternate layers.

Place the half-and-half and the cream in a saucepan and bring to a boil. Pour this mixture over the potatoes and then transfer the casserole to the oven. Bake the potatoes for about 35 minutes, or until they have absorbed most of the cream and start to brown on top. Remove from the oven and let cool for 5 minutes to let the potatoes set up before serving.

SERVES: 6 TO 8

SIMPLICITY: + +

STUFFED TWICE-BAKED POTATOES

These potatoes can be made in advance and reheated at the last minute, so they are the ideal starch for entertaining. You can even freeze them once you have stuffed them; just defrost at room temperature for 30 minutes before baking them. They are one of my wife Jody's specialties and a big hit with my family whenever they are on her menu.

2 tablespoons olive oil

1 red onion, finely diced

3 large russet potatoes, about 12 ounces each

1 tablespoon kosher salt

2 packages Boursin cheese (5.2 ounces each)

¼ cup sour cream

1 tablespoon chopped fresh chives

1 teaspoon Dijon mustard (optional)

1 large egg, beaten

Salt and freshly ground white pepper to taste

Preheat the oven to 350°F.

Heat 1 tablespoon of the oil in a skillet over medium-low heat. When the oil is hot, add the onion and sauté for 4 minutes, or until softened and just beginning to color. Remove from the heat and let cool. Rub the potatoes with the remaining 1 tablespoon olive oil and the salt and arrange in a roasting pan. Bake for 40 to 50 minutes, or until the potatoes can be pierced easily with a fork.

Remove the potatoes from the oven and cut in half lengthwise. Carefully scoop out as much of the potato flesh as you can without breaking the skin. Place the potato flesh in a bowl and add the sautéed red onion, Boursin, sour cream, chives, mustard, and egg. Mix until thoroughly incorporated and season with salt and pepper. Stuff the potato skins with the mixture and return to the roasting pan. Bake for 15 minutes, or until the tops are golden brown. Serve immediately.

CHEF'S NOTE: Large russet potatoes are often marketed as Idaho or baking potatoes. Strictly speaking, Idaho potatoes are russets grown specifically in that state, but the term is used generically to refer to any large baking potato.

SERVES: 6

SIMPLICITY: + + +

OVEN-FRIED POTATOES

Deep-frying potatoes may be most people's idea of the best way to cook the humble tuber, but it's not the healthiest, and too often, the fries come out soggy because the oil is not hot enough. With oven baking, much less oil is used and crispness is guaranteed—just be sure to serve them immediately. There's no better accompaniment for the tempura haddock on page 123.

2 pounds Idaho potatoes

2 tablespoons vegetable oil

½ tablespoon kosher salt

1 teaspoon freshly cracked black pepper

Preheat the oven to 425°F. Spray a 10 by 14-inch baking sheet with nonstick spray.

Cut the potatoes into long strips, ½ inch wide and ½ inch thick. Transfer to a bowl and toss with the oil, salt, and pepper. Arrange the potatoes on the prepared baking sheet in a single layer. Transfer to the oven and bake for 25 minutes, or until crisp and cooked through.

SERVES: 6 TO 8

SIMPLICITY: +

BAKED CHEDDAR GRITS

Until I moved to the Lone Star State, I had never tasted grits. I admit, I still haven't acquired the taste for plain grits, but as a medium for other flavors, and especially cheese, I really enjoy them. You will find this dressed-up version on winter menus at Neiman Marcus, served with roasted chicken or baked ham. In this book, I have paired it with Venison Chili (page 179). We also serve it with poached eggs for breakfast.

2 garlic cloves, crushed

1 cup corn grits (coarse or fine ground)

3 cups half-and-half or heavy cream

1 teaspoon kosher salt

1 cup grated extra-sharp Cheddar cheese

Dash of Tabasco sauce

Dash of Worcestershire sauce

Salt and freshly ground white pepper to taste

2 large eggs, separated

2 cups unseasoned dry bread crumbs

Preheat the oven to 350°F. Generously butter a 9 by 5-inch casserole dish and rub with the crushed garlic.

Place the grits and half-and-half in a small saucepan, add the salt, and bring to a simmer. Cook over medium-low heat for about 20 minutes, stirring frequently, until the grits are soft and creamy. Let the grits cool for 15 minutes and transfer to a bowl. With a rubber spatula, fold in the cheese, Tabasco, and Worcestershire sauce and season with salt and pepper. In a separate bowl, whisk the egg yolks until creamy and add them to the cooled grits mixture (the grits should be close to room temperature). In another bowl, whisk the egg whites until stiff peaks form and then fold into the grits mixture with a spatula. Pour the grits mixture into the prepared casserole, sprinkle the bread crumbs over the top, and bake for 20 minutes. Remove from the oven and spoon onto warm serving plates.

CHEF'S NOTE: When it comes to very sharp cheese, my favorite is Vermont-made Cabot Cheddar.

SERVES: 6

SIMPLICITY: + + +

WILD MUSHROOM RISOTTO

Risotto was once considered strictly restaurant fare; and it says a lot about just how far our food culture has come that more and more people feel comfortable making their own risottos at home. It requires patience and your full attention, but once mastered, the technique is straightforward and rewarding. One Mother's Day, I taught my eleven-year-old son, Patrick, to make risotto because I needed help stirring in the broth, and he got it right the first time. For a tasty appetizer, serve this dish with Gorgonzola cheese crostini (page 84).

6 cups Chicken Broth (page 267) or store-bought
  chicken stock

3 tablespoons olive oil

1 onion, minced

2 garlic cloves

1½ cups sliced button mushrooms

1½ cups sliced cremini mushrooms

1 cup Arborio rice

1 cup heavy cream

2 tablespoons unsalted butter

1 cup grated Parmesan cheese

Salt and freshly ground white pepper to taste

Pour the chicken broth into a saucepan and bring to a boil. Reduce the heat to low, keep warm, and place a heavy-bottomed saucepan on the burner directly next to it. Heat the oil in the empty saucepan over medium heat. When the oil is hot, add the onion and garlic and sauté for 3 minutes. Remove the garlic cloves, crush, and reserve. Add all of the sliced mushrooms to the pan and sauté, stirring often, for 5 minutes, or until the mushrooms are softened and have completely released their moisture. Add the rice to the pan, sauté for 1 minute, and reduce the heat to low.

Using a 4-ounce ladle or a ½-cup measure, start adding the warm chicken broth to the rice while stirring with a wooden spoon, allowing the rice to absorb each addition of liquid before adding another ladle of broth. It will take about 20 minutes for all the broth to be added and absorbed. Finally, stir in the cream, butter, cheese, and the reserved garlic. Season with salt and pepper and serve.

CHEF'S NOTE: Once the rice has absorbed all of the broth, set the risotto aside if you are not planning to serve it right away. Cover the risotto and keep for up to 1 hour on the stove. To finish the recipe, you will need to add about ½ cup water to loosen the rice while heating it over a very low flame before adding the remaining ingredients.

SERVES: 6 TO 8

SIMPLICITY: + + +

PINE NUT-STUDDED WILD RICE

Wild rice always takes me back to the days I spent in Minneapolis. I often cooked with wild rice because it is a popular side dish there. I find it goes well with most fish and poultry. Wild rice is harvested from Minnesota's boundary waters, and most people are surprised to learn that it is not rice at all but rather the seed of a long-grain marsh grass.

1 cup uncooked wild rice

1 dried bay leaf

1 chicken bouillon cube

2 tablespoons olive oil

1 small carrot, peeled and finely diced

1 celery stalk, finely diced

1 small onion, finely diced

½ cup toasted pine nuts (see page 281)

2 tablespoons chopped fresh parsley

Salt and freshly ground black pepper to taste

Pour 3 cups cold water into a saucepan and add the wild rice, bay leaf, and bouillon cube. Bring to a boil and then reduce the heat to a simmer. Cover the pan and cook over low heat for about 1 hour, or until the liquid is absorbed and the rice is tender and plump. Check the pan every 20 minutes or so to make sure the rice has not dried out; add a little more water if necessary.

Just before the rice is finished, pour the oil into a sauté pan and set over medium-high heat. When the oil is hot, add the carrot, celery, and onion and sauté for 2 minutes. Add the pine nuts, sauté for 1 minute longer, and then add the mixture to the cooked wild rice. Stir in the parsley, season with salt and pepper, and serve warm.

SERVES: 6 TO 8

SIMPLICITY: + +

SPAETZLE

Spaetzle is a traditional accompaniment, especially for red meat, that is most common in southern Germany, Alsace, Switzerland, and the Austrian Tyrol region, where it is an alternative to potatoes or rice. Some recipes suggest pressing the batter through a colander into the hot water, but I recommend you purchase a spaetzle maker at a specialty kitchen store or from an online source—the purpose-made tool makes the process a lot easier. Spaetzle is best served with foods that have sauces, as its own delicate flavor is subtle; we pair it with elk steaks and red wine sauce (page 180).

4 cups all-purpose flour

2 teaspoons kosher salt

2 teaspoons freshly ground black pepper

6 large eggs, lightly beaten

1 cup milk

¼ cup (½ stick) unsalted butter

Place the flour in a food processor fitted with a metal blade and add the salt and pepper. Add the eggs and pulse 3 or 4 times to incorporate the eggs and flour. Add the milk and blend for 10 seconds, or until the ingredients come together and form a very thick batter. Spray a rubber spatula and a bowl with nonstick spray and use the spatula to transfer the batter from the food processor to the bowl. Cover the bowl and set aside at room temperature for 1 hour.

Bring a large saucepan of salted water to a boil. Spray a spaetzle maker with nonstick spray and place over the boiling water. Using the rubber spatula and working in batches, place half of the batter in the spaetzle maker and push the batter through it into the water. After the water returns to a boil, continue to cook for 30 seconds longer; the spaetzle will float to the surface when done. Use a slotted spoon to transfer the spaetzle to a colander to drain. Place the colander under cold running water and rinse the spaetzle to stop the cooking process. Repeat for the remaining dough.

Melt the butter in a large sauté pan over medium heat. Add the spaetzle, shaking the pan frequently, and sauté for 5 minutes, or until browned slightly.

CHEF'S NOTE: Spaetzle dough is one sticky customer, so be liberal with your use of nonstick spray. It will save you much cleanup and you will have less waste, as the dough will be more reluctant to stick to everything it comes in contact with.

SERVES: 6 TO 8

SIMPLICITY: + + +

desserts

CHOCOLATE VELVET CAKE

"SOCK IT TO ME" CAKE

SHOO-FLY PIE

GRANNY SMITH APPLE PIE
   with Sharp Cheddar

PEAR GALETTES
   with Caramel Sauce and Coconut Ice Cream

CREAMY RICE PUDDING

CRUNCHY GRANOLA
   and Yogurt Berry Parfait

MAGIC SQUARES

PRINCESS HOLLYWOOD SQUARES

PECAN SUGAR BALLS

ORANGE MARMALADE COOKIES

GRISTMILL GRAHAMS

BERRIES, ICE CREAM, AND SUGAR TUILES

I'VE ALWAYS believed the art of pastry and bread-making is just that—an art. Ask any reputable professional chef the last time he or she followed a recipe, and the answer will undoubtedly be "Not since my apprenticeship." Ask the same question of a pastry chef, and the answer is likely to be "Always." Making desserts usually involves precise formulas, with no room for error. This is exactly the reason I was never very interested in the dessert section of the kitchen. I love the idea of "a little bit of this and a little bit of that" to make food taste good; patience is not a virtue I have in abundance, and taking the time to measure food precisely is not something I enjoy. For others, the opposite is true—they love working with formulas and the exactitude and discipline required to succeed. Then, one year, just before New Year's Eve, something happened that forced me to get involved in the pastry kitchen. The pastry chef at the hotel where I was executive chef went missing, and I had no choice: I had to get in there and get started on the special celebration menu. I did it all myself, and as difficult as that was, there was a silver lining: This unexpected situation forced me to overcome the block I'd had about making pastries and desserts. These were now firmly included in my repertoire.

The sampling of desserts I have chosen for this book really got me excited because I have been carrying some of them around for years; like many of the recipes in this book, they are personal favorites. Others are adapted from Helen Corbitt's recipes, and testing them all made me feel as though I was unlocking some great old forgotten favorites that fortunately now are making their way into your kitchen. My only regret, when it comes to desserts, is that much of our restaurant business at Neiman Marcus revolves around lunch, and people tend not to eat desserts then. I think most people save their sweet tooth fix for later in the day. Each of the recipes included in this chapter has been found on a Neiman Marcus menu somewhere at some time, and whether you indulge yourself at lunch, for that pick-me-up coffee break, or after dinner, I know you are going to enjoy them.

CHOCOLATE VELVET CAKE

The name Helen Corbitt gave this cake made me want to try the recipe, and I can vouch that chocolate lovers everywhere will not be disappointed. It is not your typical chocolate cake—it is dense and a little chewy but not too intense. It travels well; the frosting sets up perfectly and looks, well, good enough to eat. These qualities make it the perfect dessert to take along for a party or dinner event. Over recent years it has become a favorite of our guests at Neiman Marcus, especially for birthday celebrations.

FOR THE CAKE

1½ cups all-purpose flour, plus additional for the pans

½ cup cocoa powder

2 teaspoons baking powder

1½ teaspoons baking soda

1 teaspoon kosher salt

1¼ cups sugar

1 cup sour cream

¼ cup milk

⅓ cup vegetable oil

2 tablespoons vegetable shortening

1 teaspoon vanilla extract

2 large eggs

FOR THE FROSTING

1¾ cups heavy cream

⅓ cup dark corn syrup

16 ounces semisweet chocolate chips

Preheat the oven to 350°F. Butter and flour two 8-inch cake pans.

To prepare the cake, sift together the flour, cocoa, baking powder, baking soda, and salt into a bowl. Combine the sugar, sour cream, and milk in the bowl of an electric mixer fitted with a paddle attachment and add the oil, shortening, and vanilla. Mix on low speed for about 2 minutes, until well incorporated and smooth. Scrape down the sides of the bowl with a spatula and then add the eggs, 1 at a time. Scrape down the bowl again and add the flour and cocoa mixture in one-third increments, waiting for each addition to be incorporated before adding the next and scraping down the sides of the bowl after each addition.

Transfer the mixture to the prepared cake pans and bake in the oven for 25 to 30 minutes, or until a toothpick inserted in the center comes out clean. Let the cakes cool for 10 minutes and then turn out onto a work surface to cool completely.

While the cake is baking, prepare the frosting. Place the cream and syrup in a saucepan and bring to a boil. Place the chocolate chips in a bowl and pour the cream mixture into the chocolate, whisking until smooth. Let cool and then transfer to the bowl of an electric mixer fitted with a paddle attachment. Beat for about 4 minutes, until fluffy. Spread the frosting between the 2 layers and then frost the top and sides of the cake.

SERVES: 8

SIMPLICITY: + + +

"SOCK IT TO ME" CAKE

When I worked at the Adolphus Hotel in Dallas, just a block away on Main Street from Neiman Marcus, a member of my kitchen crew asked me if I had ever tried something called "Sock It to Me" Cake. It sounded like a joke, but after I told him I'd never had it and never even heard of it, he came in to work a few days later with this fantastic creation. It turns out to be of Southern origin, with recipes varying from one baker to the next. The name still raises eyebrows to the uninitiated—but wait until you taste this nut-studded loaf cake for the first time.

2 cups all-purpose flour, plus additional for the pan

1 teaspoon baking powder

1 teaspoon kosher salt

1 cup (2 sticks) unsalted butter, softened, plus additional for the pan

2 cups granulated sugar

½ cup light brown sugar

2 large eggs

1 cup sour cream

1 teaspoon vanilla extract

1 teaspoon ground cinnamon

½ cup chopped pecans

2 tablespoons confectioners' sugar, for dusting

Preheat the oven to 350°F. Generously butter a 9 by 6 by 4-inch loaf pan.

In a bowl, sift together the flour, baking powder, and salt and set aside. Place the butter and both types of sugar in the bowl of an electric mixer fitted with a paddle attachment and beat together on low speed for 2 minutes, until fluffy. Add the eggs, 1 at a time, and mix on medium speed for 3 minutes. Add the sour cream, vanilla, and cinnamon and then mix in the flour mixture in one-third increments, waiting for each addition to be incorporated before adding the next. Scrape down the sides of the bowl with a spatula and fold in the nuts by hand.

Transfer the mixture to the prepared loaf pan and bake in the oven for 35 to 40 minutes, or until a toothpick inserted in the center comes out clean. Let the cake cool for 15 minutes and then turn it out onto a serving platter. Sprinkle with the confectioners' sugar and serve warm or at room temperature.

SERVES: 8

SIMPLICITY: + +

SHOO-FLY PIE

Growing up 30 miles south of the Pennsylvania Dutch region, I was weaned on this early American pie at a young age, making it a childhood favorite. The name dates to the 1920s and refers to the constant shooing that must be done to keep hungry flies away from the sweet dessert. This version, in the style of a wet-bottom pie (a layer of molasses beneath a crumb topping), is adapted slightly from Helen Corbitt's original. I have to tell you we made plenty of people happy when we told them we were including Shoo-Fly Pie in this book. More than one of our guests commented that they hadn't had it in years, since their grandma made it. I see no reason not to make this old favorite to share with family and friends today.

FOR THE PIE DOUGH

1½ cups all-purpose flour

½ cup (1 stick) unsalted butter

½ teaspoon salt

½ teaspoon sugar

½ tablespoon white vinegar

1 large egg yolk

3 tablespoons ice water

FOR THE PIE FILLING

½ teaspoon baking soda

½ teaspoon dark molasses

Streusel Crumb Topping (page 40)

To prepare the pie dough, combine the flour, butter, salt, sugar, vinegar, and egg yolk in a food processor. Process together briefly and then pulse in the ice water until the dough becomes mealy in consistency. Turn out on a floured work surface, knead briefly to bring the dough together, and wrap in a sheet of plastic wrap. Transfer to the refrigerator and let chill for at least 1 hour or overnight.

Preheat the oven to 375°F.

To prepare the filling, pour ½ cup water into a saucepan and bring to a boil. Add the baking soda and molasses and stir together. Remove the pan from the heat and add two thirds of the crumb topping. Mix with a rubber spatula until well incorporated. Set aside.

Remove the pie dough from the refrigerator and roll into a 10-inch circle. Transfer to a 9-inch pie tin and crimp the edges to form the crust. Return to the refrigerator for 10 to 15 minutes to set up before filling.

Pour the filling into the pie shell and sprinkle the remaining one-third crumb mixture on top of the pie. Bake for 35 to 40 minutes, or until the crust and crumb topping are golden brown. Remove from the oven and let sit for 10 minutes to set up. Serve warm, with a dollop of whipped cream, if desired.

SERVES: 8

SIMPLICITY: + + +

GRANNY SMITH APPLE PIE
with Sharp Cheddar

I first tasted apple pie with cheese when I worked in Stowe, Vermont, in the late 1970s. Fitting in with the local custom and practice, I learned to appreciate the way a good sharp cheese cuts through a sweet fruit pie and complements it perfectly. I've served apple pie with cheese ever since, because the tradition—not widely known outside New England—deserves a wider audience.

Pie Dough (page 221, Shoo-Fly Pie)

Streusel Crumb Topping (page 40)

FOR THE PIE FILLING

5 Granny Smith apples, peeled, cored, and cut into
    thin (⅛-inch) slices

1 cup granulated sugar

1 large egg, beaten

½ teaspoon ground cinnamon

½ teaspoon grated lemon zest

⅛ teaspoon kosher salt

1 teaspoon vanilla extract

¼ cup light brown sugar

2 tablespoons unsalted butter, softened

4 ounces sharp Cheddar cheese, cut into 8 slices

Prepare the pie dough and refrigerate. Prepare the crumb topping.

Preheat the oven to 400°F.

Remove the pie dough from the refrigerator and roll into a 10-inch circle. Transfer to a 9-inch pie tin and crimp the edges to form the crust. Return to the refrigerator for 10 to 15 minutes to set up before filling.

To make the filling, combine the apples, granulated sugar, egg, cinnamon, lemon zest, salt, vanilla, brown sugar, and butter in a bowl. Add ½ cup of the crumb topping and fold together to thoroughly incorporate. Spoon the filling into the pie shell and cover evenly with the remaining crumb topping. Transfer to the oven and bake for about 40 minutes, or until the crust and crumb topping are golden brown.

Remove the pie from the oven and let it sit for 10 minutes to set up before serving. Place a slice of pie on each serving plate and top with a slice of the cheese.

SERVES: 8

SIMPLICITY: + + +

PEAR GALETTES
with Caramel Sauce and Coconut Ice Cream

I learned to make fruit galettes from Jean Banchet, the renowned former chef and owner of the acclaimed restaurant Le Français in Wheeling, Illinois. Banchet was the consulting chef at the Adolphus Hotel in Dallas when I was the executive chef there, and the galette was a popular dessert in the hotel's French Room restaurant. I have used this recipe ever since, and I love that this elegant, simple dessert is straightforward and uncomplicated to make. You can use Granny Smith apples instead of the pears, if you wish, or ripe fresh peaches or plums during summer.

FOR THE COCONUT ICE CREAM

1 cup heavy cream

1 cup milk

¾ cup sugar

3 large eggs, beaten

1 can (15 ounces) Coco Lopez cream of coconut

1 cup sweetened shredded coconut

FOR THE CARAMEL SAUCE

1 cup light brown sugar

½ cup granulated sugar

½ cup light corn syrup

1 cup heavy cream

Juice of ½ lemon

1 tablespoon unsalted butter

FOR THE PEAR GALETTES

1 sheet frozen puff pastry

6 teaspoons almond paste

6 firm Bartlett or Anjou pears, peeled, cored, and
  cut in half

3 teaspoons sugar

3 teaspoons unsalted butter

To prepare the ice cream, pour the cream and milk into a saucepan and bring to a boil over medium heat. Meanwhile, whisk together the sugar and eggs in a bowl until pale in color. Slowly pour the hot milk mixture into the egg mixture, whisking constantly. Pour the entire mixture back into the saucepan and cook over medium heat, stirring constantly with a wooden spoon, for about 5 minutes, or until the mixture thickens slightly. Strain into a bowl and set the bowl in a larger bowl containing ice water to cool. When the mixture has completely cooled, whisk in the cream of coconut and shredded coconut. Transfer the mixture to an ice cream maker and follow the manufacturer's directions for freezing. Once the ice cream is frozen, scoop it into a container, cover, and transfer to the freezer until ready to serve.

To prepare the caramel sauce, combine the brown sugar, granulated sugar, and corn syrup in a saucepan and bring to a boil over high heat. Continue to cook until the mixture begins to brown, about 10 minutes. Remove the pan from the heat and whisk in the cream, lemon juice, and butter until smooth. Let cool before serving. The sauce can be refrigerated and brought to room temperature before serving.

Preheat the oven to 400°F.

To prepare the galettes, use a knife to cut out 6 circles of puff pastry, each about 5 inches across. Place each puff pastry disk on a clean work surface. Spread 1 teaspoon of the almond paste on each disk, leaving a ¼-inch border of exposed puff pastry. Slice each pear half into thin slices and fan out slightly on top of each puff pastry disk. Sprinkle each pear half with ½ teaspoon sugar and top with ½ teaspoon butter. Place the pear galettes on a baking sheet and transfer to the oven. Bake for 12 minutes, or until golden brown.

To serve, remove the galettes from the baking sheet and arrange on serving plates. Spoon some of the sauce onto the plates and top each warm galette with a scoop of ice cream.

SERVES: 6

SIMPLICITY: + + + +

CREAMY RICE PUDDING

This is one of those special-occasion recipes my mom used to make when important company was coming to the house. She always used little ovenproof pudding cups that I wish I had today. Over the years, I've relaxed the criteria for making this dessert and prepare it whenever the fancy strikes. Of course, Mom always wanted it served warm from the oven, but at my house, we prefer it the day after it's made, served straight from the refrigerator with lots of whipped cream.

1 cup raisins

1 tablespoon dark rum or water

5 cups milk

1½ cups plus 1 tablespoon sugar

¼ teaspoon kosher salt

1 vanilla bean, split in half, or 1 teaspoon vanilla
　　extract

1 cup long-grain white rice

1½ cups heavy cream

3 large eggs

½ teaspoon ground cinnamon

Preheat the oven to 375°F. Butter eight to ten 6-ounce ramekins.

Put the raisins in a bowl, add the rum, and let the raisins soak while you cook the rice.

Pour the milk into a saucepan and add 1½ cups of the sugar, the salt, vanilla bean, and rice. (If using vanilla extract, add it later.) Bring to a boil over medium heat. Reduce the heat to low, cover the pan, and cook for about 35 minutes, stirring often, or until the rice is tender. Turn off the heat and let cool. If using vanilla extract, add it now.

Bring about 4 cups water to a boil in a teakettle or a saucepan.

In a bowl, whisk together 1 cup of the cream and the eggs. When the rice is cool, remove the vanilla bean and stir in the egg mixture and the raisins soaked in rum (add any rum left in the bowl, if you wish). Pour the rice mixture into the prepared ramekins. In a cup, mix together the cinnamon and the remaining 1 tablespoon sugar and sprinkle over the rice puddings. Place the ramekins in a small roasting pan, transfer to the oven, and pour boiling water into the pan so it comes halfway up the sides of the ramekins. Bake for about 30 minutes, or until the custard is set. Whip the remaining ½ cup cream and garnish each serving with a dollop of the whipped cream. Serve warm, at room temperature, or chilled.

SERVES: 8 TO 10

SIMPLICITY: + + +

CRUNCHY GRANOLA
and Yogurt Berry Parfait

Everyone should make homemade granola at least once. I guarantee that after experiencing the wonderful aromas from the oven and then marveling at how well the flavors came together, you'll want to make it again and again. This granola recipe yields a total of about 10 cups, of which you will use 4 cups for the parfait. It takes some time to assemble everything and prepare, but it's well worth it, and because making a big batch takes just as long as a small batch, you may as well make extra to savor at breakfast or to fill Mason jars and give as gifts. After making granola a few times, you'll start to add and subtract ingredients; pretty soon you'll have your own house version.

FOR THE CRUNCHY GRANOLA

4 cups old-fashioned rolled oats (not instant oats)

2 cups sweetened shredded coconut

2 cups slivered almonds

1½ teaspoons ground cinnamon

½ cup honey

½ cup light brown sugar

1 cup vegetable oil

1 teaspoon vanilla extract

3 cups mixed dried fruit, such as raisins, cranberries, blueberries, cherries, and chopped apricots

1 cup unsalted cashews, pistachios, or macadamia nuts (optional)

FOR THE PARFAITS

3 cups assorted berries, such as quartered strawberries or whole blueberries, raspberries, or blackberries

3 cups low-fat or regular vanilla yogurt

6 fresh mint leaves (optional)

Preheat the oven to 300°F. Spray two 11 by 17-inch baking sheets with nonstick spray.

To prepare the granola, place the oats in a bowl, add the coconut, almonds, and cinnamon, and thoroughly combine. In a separate bowl, whisk together the honey, brown sugar, oil, and vanilla, and then pour this mixture into the dry ingredients. Stir together with a wooden spoon until completely incorporated. Spread this mixture evenly onto the prepared baking sheets and transfer to the oven. Bake for 20 to 25 minutes, or until light golden brown, stirring the granola with a wooden spoon every 5 to 7 minutes. Remove from the oven and let the granola cool for 5 minutes. Transfer to a large clean bowl and mix in the dried fruits and nuts, if using; the mixture should clump together lightly. Once cool, store in an airtight container at room temperature (it does not need to be refrigerated).

To prepare the parfaits, place ¼ cup assorted berries in the bottom of each of 6 parfait glasses. Add ⅓ cup granola and top with ¼ cup yogurt per glass. Repeat the layers and garnish each parfait with a mint leaf.

CHEF NOTES: Make the parfaits about 30 minutes before serving so the layers have a chance to mingle while still remaining distinct in the glasses. The granola will keep for up to 2 weeks before losing some of its flavor.

YIELD: 6 PARFAITS

SIMPLICITY: + +

MAGIC SQUARES

My life changed for the better when I first tasted these delicious morsels at the Woodstock Inn in Woodstock, Vermont, when I worked there as executive chef. I knew at once I had to have the recipe, so I asked Bunny, the pastry chef who had worked there for forty-five years and who was on the verge of retirement. I like to think of these sweet squares as a great pick-me-up bite to enjoy with that afternoon coffee fix.

1½ cups (3 sticks) unsalted butter, melted

3 cups graham cracker crumbs

2 cups semisweet chocolate chips

2 cups unsalted peanuts

1½ cups unsweetened shredded coconut

2 cans (14 ounces each) sweetened condensed milk

Preheat the oven to 350°F.

In a bowl, thoroughly combine the butter and cracker crumbs. Transfer to a rimmed 11 by 17-inch baking sheet and spread out evenly. Sprinkle the chocolate chips evenly over the mixture, then add the peanuts in an even layer, and, finally, the coconut. Pour the condensed milk over the ingredients.

Transfer to the oven and bake for about 25 minutes, or until the top is slightly golden brown. Remove from the oven, let cool, and cut into squares slightly larger than 2 inches (the pan should contain 5 squares along the short side, 8 squares on the long side).

CHEF'S NOTE: Store uneaten squares in an airtight container at room temperature. They will keep for up to 1 week, or in the freezer for up to 1 month.

YIELD: ABOUT 40 SQUARES

SIMPLICITY: +

PRINCESS HOLLYWOOD SQUARES

These squares also originated at the Woodstock Inn (see page 232). They are the perfect sweet served with afternoon tea and get their princess pink interior from raspberry preserves. At Neiman Marcus, we serve these squares in the fall and during the holiday season as an after-lunch treat; in fact, they have become quite a signature item.

4 cups unsweetened shredded coconut

3½ cups all-purpose flour

3 cups sugar

3 cups vegetable shortening

1½ cups chopped walnuts

2 large eggs, beaten

2½ cups raspberry preserves

Preheat the oven to 350°F. Spray a rimmed 11 by 17-inch baking sheet with nonstick spray.

Combine the coconut, flour, sugar, shortening, walnuts, and eggs in the bowl of an electric mixer fitted with a paddle attachment. Mix on medium speed for 4 minutes, or until fluffy. Spread half of the dough mixture evenly on the prepared baking sheet, using a spatula. Spread the preserves evenly over the mixture and then cover with the remaining dough mix.

Transfer to the oven and bake for 30 minutes, or until the dough resembles a soft-baked cookie. Remove from the oven and let cool; the dough will firm up when completely cooled. Cut into squares slightly larger than 2 inches (the pan should contain 5 squares along the short side, 8 squares on the long side).

CHEF'S NOTE: Store uneaten squares in an airtight container at room temperature. They will keep for up to 1 week, or in the freezer for up to 1 month.

YIELD: ABOUT 40 SQUARES

SIMPLICITY: +

PECAN SUGAR BALLS

This is a great last-minute recipe, and because you can make a lot very quickly, these pecan balls make a good party dish or gift. You will find similar cookies in countries as diverse as Italy and Mexico, where the balls (called "wedding cookies") are rolled in a cinnamon-sugar mixture. Pecans are plentiful in Texas during the fall each year, and this is a great way of putting them to good use.

1 pound (4 sticks) butter, softened, plus additional
    for the baking sheet

1 cup confectioners' sugar, sifted, plus ¼ cup for
    dusting

4½ cups cake flour

2 cups chopped pecans

2 teaspoons vanilla extract

Preheat the oven to 300°F. Lightly butter an 11 by 17-inch baking sheet.

In the bowl of an electric mixer fitted with a paddle attachment, cream the butter, sugar, flour, pecans, and vanilla for 2 or 3 minutes, or until all the ingredients are well mixed. Remove the mixture from the bowl and transfer to a floured work surface. Form the mixture into a large ball and then, using your fingers or a small scoop, shape into 36 little half-balls and place on the prepared baking sheet. Transfer to the oven and bake for 30 minutes, or until the cookies are dry in the middle.

Remove the pecan sugar balls from the baking sheet and let cool on a wire rack. Dust with the ¼ cup of confectioners' sugar before serving.

CHEF'S NOTE: These cookies keep better undusted. Store in an airtight container at room temperature for 1 week, or in the freezer for up to 1 month.

YIELD: 36 COOKIES

SIMPLICITY: +

ORANGE MARMALADE COOKIES

Iced cookies are so simple and satisfying, they should be baked at home as often as chocolate chip cookies. To that end, I have brought back a great Helen Corbitt recipe to share with everyone. The secret is to ice the cookies when they have completely cooled; that way, you can spread a thick layer of icing that sets up well and will not smear.

FOR THE COOKIES

3 cups all-purpose flour

½ teaspoon baking soda

½ teaspoon salt

½ cup vegetable shortening or unsalted butter, plus additional butter for the cookie sheet

1 cup sugar

2 large eggs, beaten

1 cup orange marmalade

FOR THE ORANGE ICING

2 teaspoons grated orange zest

1 teaspoon grated lemon zest

¼ cup freshly squeezed orange juice

1 teaspoon freshly squeezed lemon juice

3 tablespoons unsalted butter, softened

3 cups confectioners' sugar

⅛ teaspoon kosher salt

Preheat the oven to 300°F. Generously butter a cookie sheet.

To prepare the cookies, sift together the flour, baking soda, and salt into a bowl and set aside. Place the shortening in the bowl of an electric mixer fitted with a paddle attachment and beat on low speed. Add the sugar and continue beating for about 2 minutes, until light and fluffy. Add the eggs and mix well. Add the reserved dry ingredients and the marmalade and mix thoroughly. Remove the bowl from the mixer and, using a teaspoon, drop the cookie dough onto the prepared cookie sheet. Transfer to the oven and bake for about 20 minutes, or until the cookies are light brown in color.

While the cookies are baking, prepare the icing. Combine the orange and lemon zests and juices in a bowl. In the bowl of an electric mixer fitted with a paddle attachment, beat the butter on low speed. Add 1 cup of the confectioners' sugar and blend thoroughly. Add the remaining 2 cups sugar, the salt, and the citrus juice mixture and blend until smooth.

Remove the cookies from the oven and transfer to a wire rack to cool. When cooled, ice the cookies with a palette knife or a butter knife.

YIELD: ABOUT 36 COOKIES

SIMPLICITY: + +

GRISTMILL GRAHAMS

I love this Helen Corbitt recipe, which uses graham flour made from coarsely ground whole wheat. If you are unable to find graham flour—introduced in the first half of the nineteenth century by Sylvester Graham, an American Presbyterian minister and physician who advocated vegetarianism, abstinence, and a healthy diet—use whole-wheat flour instead. You'll be doing a better job than some producers of commercial graham crackers who use refined, bleached white flour and colorings, to which Dr. Graham was adamantly opposed.

¾ cup vegetable shortening

1 cup dark brown sugar

½ cup sugar

2 large eggs

2 cups all-purpose flour

1 teaspoon baking soda

1 teaspoon kosher salt

1 cup graham flour or whole-wheat flour, sifted

1 teaspoon grated nutmeg

1 cup dates, pitted and minced

2 teaspoons vanilla extract

½ cup confectioners' sugar, for dusting

Preheat the oven to 375°F. Lightly butter an 11 by 17-inch baking sheet.

In the bowl of an electric mixer fitted with a paddle attachment, beat the shortening with the brown and granulated sugars on low speed for 3 to 4 minutes, until light and fluffy. Add the eggs, 1 at a time, while beating, and when they are incorporated, add the all-purpose flour, baking soda, and salt. Add the graham flour, nutmeg, dates, and vanilla. Continue mixing together for about 5 minutes, until all of the ingredients are well blended.

Transfer the dough to the prepared baking sheet. Pat out the dough with your knuckles so it fits in an even layer and into the corners of the pan. Score the surface of the dough with a sharp knife to form 2-inch squares. Use a fork to prick each bar 3 or 4 times. Sprinkle the top with the confectioners' sugar and transfer to the oven. Bake for 12 to 15 minutes, until the dough is puffed up and lightly browned. Remove from the oven and let cool in the pan for 15 min-utes. When they are cool enough to handle, cut out the bars into the scored 2-inch squares.

YIELD: ABOUT 40 BARS

SIMPLICITY: + +

Presentation is everything when it comes to serving guests in your home. Helen Corbitt was dubbed "the queen of the ladies' lunch" by James Beard, and not just because she served great food; she also created a fabulous setting for her guests. This recipe—berries and ice cream nestled in a cookie basket—scores high marks for both flavor and style.

Coconut Ice Cream (page 226) or store-bought
    chocolate ice cream

FOR THE BERRIES

1 cup fresh strawberries, hulled and quartered

1 cup fresh raspberries, blackberries, or
    blueberries

1 tablespoon brandy or orange liqueur

1 tablespoon light brown sugar

¼ cup chopped fresh mint leaves

¼ teaspoon freshly ground black pepper

FOR THE TUILES

½ cup (1 stick) unsalted butter

¾ cup light brown sugar

½ cup light corn syrup

½ cup plus 2 tablespoons all-purpose flour

Prepare the ice cream.

Preheat the oven to 350°F.

Wash and dry the berries and place in a small stainless-steel or nonreactive bowl. Sprinkle the brandy and sugar over the berries and gently mix, using a spatula. Add the mint, sprinkle with the pepper, and mix again. Cover the bowl with plastic wrap and refrigerate for 1 hour to chill.

To prepare the tuiles, combine the butter, sugar, and corn syrup in a saucepan and bring to a boil. Boil for just 15 seconds and then remove from the heat. Whisk in the flour until incorporated into the mixture. Pour the mixture through a large-hole strainer onto a baking sheet and spread out evenly with a spatula to cool.

Line an 11 by 17-inch baking sheet with parchment paper. When the tuile mixture is cool enough to handle, pull off a small piece and form into a ball about the size of a small Ping-Pong ball. Place the ball on the prepared baking sheet and repeat with the remaining mixture. Leave 4 to 5 inches between the balls so they have enough room to spread when baked.

Transfer to the oven and bake for about 8 minutes, or until the tuile mixture flattens out and begins to brown. While the tuiles are baking, set 6 to 8 tumblers, cups, or small serving dishes on a work surface; these will be inverted and used to shape the tuiles. Remove the tuiles from the oven and carefully slide the parchment paper off the baking sheet and onto a clean work surface. Flip the parchment paper so the tuiles are lying on the work surface. Using a spatula, carefully lift each warm tuile and drape over the bottom of the tumblers, cups, or small serving dishes to form little basket shapes. Let cool completely before removing the tuiles and setting right side up.

When ready to serve, place the tuile baskets on plates and garnish with ice cream and the berry mixture.

CHEF'S NOTE: The caramel sauce on page 226 works very well with this combination.

SERVES: 6 TO 8

SIMPLICITY: + + +

cocktails

and beverages

AS I WAS researching recipes in the Neiman Marcus archives, I came across a few drink recipes, both with and without alcohol, that caught my eye and helped me decide we really needed to include a chapter on them in this book. We have only a handful of stores with full-service bars—the Neiman Marcus properties in Coral Gables, Beverly Hills, San Francisco, and Honolulu—but the archives are overflowing with colorful and flavorful ideas for drinks and nonalcoholic beverages. I was amazed at the simplicity, and also the creativity, of these drink recipes, many of which date to parties and events held at Neiman Marcus decades ago. So much of what we do in our restaurants to this day involves special events: celebrations, new fashion launch parties, large city fund-raisers, personal appearances by designers. Each event has a theme that dictates what food and beverages are served. I hope you enjoy these drinks at your next event and keep them handy for special occasions. I know I'll be putting my new favorites back in circulation at Neiman Marcus as well as at home!

MARIPOSA COCKTAIL

I was excited to find this recipe named after the Mariposa from the early Helen Corbitt recipe files, as many of our restaurants now bear this name. After some reworking, I introduced this cocktail into our Florida stores, and it soon became a huge hit. Don't be put off by the fruit garnish; it's always a good thing to have a little fruit with your cocktails—it makes them so much healthier!

2 tablespoons brandy

1 tablespoon dark rum

1 tablespoon freshly squeezed orange juice

1 tablespoon freshly squeezed lemon juice

2 teaspoons grenadine

1 maraschino cherry, for garnish

1 strawberry, hulled, for garnish

Fill a tall highball glass with ice. Pour in the brandy, rum, orange juice, lemon juice, and grenadine. Put the cherry and strawberry on a cocktail skewer and garnish the glass with the skewer.

SERVES: 1

HELEN CORBITT COOKS FOR COOKS

251

TEA AND WHISKEY TODDY

On my last trip to Ireland, I fell in love with this simple drink. The Irish serve a shot of poteen (Irish homemade whiskey) in a tall, clear coffee mug and fill it up with hot tea; then they drop a sugar cube into the glass. I've gone ahead and dressed it up with the addition of mint-flavored simple syrup instead of the sugar cube. I also favor freshly brewed blackcurrant tea, but feel free to use your favorite kind. You won't find poteen at your local liquor store, so choose a good Irish whiskey for this warming cocktail.

FOR THE MINT-FLAVORED SIMPLE SYRUP

½ cup sugar

1 bunch fresh mint, leaves only

FOR THE TODDY

⅔ cup freshly brewed blackcurrant tea or other
    hot tea of your choice

3 tablespoons Irish whiskey

1 lemon slice, for garnish

To prepare the simple syrup, bring 1 cup water to a boil in a small saucepan and add the sugar and mint leaves. Turn off the heat, stir to dissolve the sugar, and let the mint leaves sit in the syrup for 1 hour. Strain the syrup, discarding the mint leaves, and store the syrup in an airtight container in the refrigerator.

To prepare the toddy, pour the tea into your favorite mug or a tall glass. Warm the whiskey in the microwave for 30 seconds and add it to the tea. Stir in 1 tablespoon of the simple syrup. Garnish with the lemon slice.

CHEF'S NOTE: The mint-flavored simple syrup will keep for up to 1 month. It also makes a great flavoring for iced tea.

SERVES: 1

EGGNOG CREAM

This was a last-minute recipe I created during the holiday season one year when a group of guests requested eggnog. Not having any on hand, I was forced to improvise. My first thought was to whip up a thick vanilla crème anglaise, but without the luxury of time, I chose to use vanilla ice cream as the base. I added yolks and sugar to make it thicker and creamier, and a legend was born. Every holiday season since then my regular customers and friends have asked me to prepare the recipe.

¼ cup brandy

1 cup bourbon

1 cup sugar

½ cup pasteurized egg yolks (about 5 large eggs)

1 quart vanilla ice cream, softened

¼ teaspoon ground cinnamon

¼ teaspoon grated nutmeg

Pour the brandy, bourbon, and sugar into a cocktail shaker and shake vigorously to dissolve the sugar. Let sit for 1 hour to allow the flavors to come together.

In the bowl of an electric mixer fitted with a paddle attachment, beat the egg yolks on medium speed for 7 or 8 minutes, until thick and creamy. Add the reserved liquor mixture and beat in the ice cream and the cinnamon. Chill in the refrigerator for 2 hours before serving. Pour into rocks or double old-fashioned glasses and sprinkle nutmeg over each drink.

CHEF'S NOTE: Pasteurized egg yolks are available at some supermarkets and specialty grocery stores. If you can't find them, use regular egg yolks, provided you do not have a compromised immune system.

SERVES: 8

SANGRIA À LA CORDOBA

Sangria is a refreshing wine punch that hails from Spain. Its name comes from the Spanish word for "blood," referring to its ruby red color, although chilled white wine can also be used—in which case the drink is properly called sangria blanca. *There are no limits to the type of fruit that can be used—go with your own preferences and whatever is in season.*

1 pint fresh strawberries

1 orange, peeled and sliced

½ lemon, peeled and sliced

1 pint fresh raspberries

1 peach, pitted and thinly sliced

⅓ cup orange liqueur

¼ cup brandy

½ cup freshly squeezed orange juice

1 bottle (750 mL) red wine, preferably Rioja

Reserve 6 strawberries for garnish, making a small incision in the pointed end so they can be placed on the rim of the wineglasses. Hull and quarter the remaining strawberries and place in a large pitcher together with the orange and lemon slices. Add the raspberries and sliced peach and pour in the orange liqueur, brandy, and orange juice. Cover the pitcher and chill in the refrigerator for I hour.

Just before serving, add the wine and stir well. Fill wineglasses with plenty of ice and strain the sangria into them. Garnish each glass with a reserved strawberry.

CHEF'S NOTE: You can serve some of the macerated fruit if you'd like, but you will need large wineglasses.

SERVES: 6

When an autumnal chill is in the air and the apple harvest begins, there is nothing quite as satisfying as hot apple cider. When I lived in New England, freshly squeezed apple cider was one of the seasonal ingredients I looked forward to the most. I like to serve a plate of Gristmill Grahams (page 240) with this warming brew.

1 quart fresh apple cider

1 tablespoon light brown sugar

1 cinnamon stick

1 teaspoon cloves

1 teaspoon ground allspice

⅛ teaspoon ground mace

Pinch of kosher salt

Pinch of cayenne pepper

Combine the apple cider, sugar, cinnamon, cloves, allspice, mace, salt, and cayenne in a large saucepan and bring just to a simmer, stirring occasionally. Reduce the heat to low and simmer for 2 minutes. Remove from the heat and let sit for 1 hour to macerate.

Strain the mixture into a clean saucepan (discard the solids) and return to a simmer. Serve warm in tall coffee mugs.

SERVES: 6

ORANGE-GINGER ALE PUNCH

This is a great drink to serve at large gatherings of family or friends. Kids and adults alike will enjoy your effort to make such a simple concoction look fun and taste refreshing.

3 cups plus 1 tablespoon freshly squeezed orange
   juice
1 tablespoon sugar
2 cans (12 ounces each) ginger ale
1 orange, cut into 6 thin slices, for garnish
6 maraschino cherries, for garnish
6 fresh mint sprigs, for garnish

Pour 1½ cups of the orange juice into ice cube trays and freeze.

Place the sugar on a small plate and pour the 1 tablespoon orange juice onto a small saucer or another plate. Dip 6 glasses into the orange juice and then into the sugar so it sticks to the rim. Divide the orange juice cubes among the glasses and pour in the 1½ cups orange juice and the ginger ale. Garnish each glass with an orange slice, a cherry, and a mint sprig.

CHEF'S NOTE: You will need to prepare ahead by freezing the orange juice in ice cube trays. This is a great technique to use for other punches and mixed drinks so they don't get watered down by regular ice.

SERVES: 6

HOT CRANAPPLE PUNCH

As the name suggests, cranapple juice is a sweet-tart blend of cranberry and apple juices that dates commercially to the 1950s. This warming punch recipe celebrates the fall and winter seasons.

1 cup cranapple juice

¼ cup water

½ teaspoon light brown sugar

1 cinnamon stick

2 cloves

Pinch of kosher salt

Combine the juice, water, sugar, cinnamon, cloves, and salt in a tall glass and heat in the microwave for about 2 minutes, or until hot. Stir well to make sure the sugar and salt are dissolved; there is no need to strain, although you can if you prefer.

SERVES: 1

MOCK PINK CHAMPAGNE

In recent years, pink champagne has made a big comeback, with people accepting it as a prestigious way to enjoy champagne. The French, who developed the champagne grape and its marriage with pinot noir to make pink champagne, have long loved the color and slightly sweet taste of this bubbling magic. Here we throw out all classic fine tastes and enjoy our version as a pure nonalcoholic winner. If you have champagne taste and a lemon–lime soda budget, you are in for a treat.

½ cup simple syrup (see Chef's Note)

3 cups cranberry juice

1½ cups pineapple juice

18 cranberries (about 1 cup), for garnish

1½ cups (1 can) lemon-lime soda (such as Sprite)

In a pitcher, mix the simple syrup with the cranberry juice and pineapple juice and chill in the refrigerator for 1 hour. Place 3 cranberries in each of six 8-ounce champagne glasses and pour ¾ cup of the juice mixture into each glass. Top with ¼ cup of the soda and serve immediately.

CHEF'S NOTE: For the simple syrup, make the recipe on page 252, but omit the mint.

SERVES: 6

CHILLED COFFEE FLOAT

I recall the aroma of fresh brewed coffee wafting from the kitchen when I was growing up, opening up the house each morning with a welcoming smell. Believe it or not, Helen Corbitt created this recipe for children, and the early version of the recipe called for Sanka, the only decaffeinated offering in the 1950s and '60s. No doubt her version was sweeter than most, but I bet the kids felt so grown up!

1 cup strong brewed coffee, chilled

Sugar to taste (optional)

Dash of vanilla extract

2 scoops vanilla ice cream, softened

1 tablespoon whipped heavy cream

Pour the coffee into a tall glass; sweeten, if desired, and add the vanilla. Float the ice cream on top of the coffee and top with the whipped cream.

SERVES: 1

basics

sauces, and condiments

ASK ANY CHEF what he or she feels is the most important aspect of cooking; the answer will be that a strong knowledge of the basics—the proper preparation of sauces and stocks and a mastery of essential cooking techniques such as sautéing, grilling, and roasting—is essential. Without understanding these fundamentals, a cook can never hope to wow either customers or guests. So here are some of my go-to flavor building blocks in the kitchen. When you add these recipes to your repertoire, you will be able to elevate your cooking to a higher level.

VEGETABLE BROTH

This broth is deliberately lacking salt and pepper so you can adjust the flavors once you decide how you will use it. Because this is a neutral-tasting stock, it can be adapted for many purposes; use it as a substitute for chicken or beef broth, especially if you want to make a vegetarian dish. Freeze it in small batches so you will not have to defrost all of it whenever you want to use it.

2 white onions, cut into large dice

2 ripe tomatoes, cut into large dice

1 leek, trimmed, green and white parts cut into large dice

2 carrots, peeled and cut into large dice

4 celery stalks, cut into large dice

1 zucchini, cut into large dice

10 button mushrooms, quartered

½ bunch fresh parsley

6 sprigs fresh thyme

Pour 6 quarts cold water into a stockpot and add the onions, tomatoes, leek, carrots, celery, zucchini, mushrooms, parsley, and thyme. There should be enough water to cover the ingredients by at least 2 inches; add more water if necessary. Bring to a boil, reduce the heat to low, and partially cover with a lid. Simmer gently for 1 hour, skimming the surface occasionally to remove any impurities. Strain into clean containers through a fine strainer and discard the solids.

CHEF'S NOTE: Store the broth in airtight containers. It will keep for up to 1 week in the refrigerator and up to 1 month in the freezer.

YIELD: ABOUT 4 QUARTS

SIMPLICITY: +

CHICKEN BROTH

This broth plays an important role in Neiman Marcus kitchens across the country. It not only forms the basis of many soups, stews, and sauces but also is served as a complimentary demitasse for all our guests to begin their meal. This is a tradition that has continued ever since the 1950s, when Stanley Marcus ("Mr. Stanley") proposed this gesture of hospitality to Helen Corbitt.

5 pounds mixed chicken parts

1 large onion, chopped

8 celery stalks, chopped

1 large carrot, peeled and chopped

3 garlic cloves

5 black peppercorns

1 dried bay leaf

3 fresh thyme sprigs

1 bunch fresh parsley, stems only

2 chicken bouillon cubes, crumbled

Rinse the chicken pieces under cold running water and place in a heavy-bottomed stockpot. Add the onion, celery, carrot, garlic, peppercorns, bay leaf, thyme, parsley, and bouillon cubes and about 2 gallons cold water, or enough to cover the ingredients by about 2 inches. Bring to a boil, reduce the heat to low, and partially cover with a lid. Simmer for about 1 hour, skimming the surface occasionally to remove fat and impurities.

Remove the cooked chicken, let cool, and remove the poached meat from the bones; reserve for another use. Return the bones to the stockpot and continue to simmer for 2 hours longer. Strain into clean containers through a fine strainer and discard the bones and the solids.

CHEF'S NOTE: Store the broth in airtight containers. It will keep for up to 1 week in the refrigerator and up to 1 month in the freezer.

YIELD: ABOUT 3 QUARTS

SIMPLICITY: + +

BEEF BROTH

Save leftover beef bones from steaks, prime rib roast, and other cuts on an ongoing basis and freeze them. When you have enough, you can make this broth. If you need to ask your butcher for bones, ask for ones containing marrow, which will give the broth body and lots of flavor. This broth freezes well; do so in small batches to make using it more practical.

10 pounds beef bones

2 onions, cut into large dice

2 large carrots, peeled, cut into large dice

4 celery stalks, cut into large dice

6 garlic cloves

1 cup canned tomatoes, diced, with juice

2 dried bay leaves

6 black peppercorns

4 sprigs fresh thyme

6 sprigs fresh parsley

½ cup dry red wine

Preheat the oven to 375°F.

Place the beef bones in 1 or 2 large roasting pans and roast in the oven for 30 minutes. Add the onions, carrots, celery, garlic, tomatoes, bay leaves, peppercorns, thyme, and parsley to the pan (divide evenly if using 2 pans) and continue roasting for 30 minutes longer, turning the bones as needed to ensure they are completely browned along with the vegetables.

Remove from the oven, pour in the wine, and deglaze the pan by scraping the bottom with a wooden spoon to loosen any solids. Let cool a little before transferring the ingredients to a stockpot. Cover the bones and vegetables with 2 gallons cold water or enough to cover the ingredients by 5 inches. Bring to a boil, reduce the heat to low, and partially cover with a lid. Simmer gently for 2 hours, skimming the surface occasionally to remove fat and impurities.

Strain into clean containers through a fine strainer and discard the solids.

CHEF'S NOTE: Store the broth in airtight containers. It will keep for up to 1 week in the refrigerator and up to 1 month in the freezer.

YIELD: ABOUT 4 QUARTS

SIMPLICITY: + +

TOMATO SAUCE

All home cooks seem to have their own tomato sauce recipe, and this is mine. The key is to use the best canned tomatoes you can find; I prefer brands from Italy. I use this sauce for Eggplant Parmesan (page 195), and of course you can serve it over cooked pasta any time.

2 tablespoons olive oil

1 onion, finely diced

2 garlic cloves, crushed

1 large can (28 ounces) peeled and diced tomatoes

1 can (14 ounces) tomato purée

6 fresh basil leaves, minced

2 chicken bouillon cubes

Pour the olive oil into a large saucepan and set over medium-low heat. When the oil is hot, add the onion and garlic and sauté for 8 minutes, or until soft. Add the tomatoes and tomato purée and increase the heat to medium-high. Bring to a boil and then reduce the heat to low. Add the basil and bouillon cubes and simmer the sauce for 30 minutes, stirring occasionally.

CHEF'S NOTE: Store the sauce in an airtight container for up to 3 days in the refrigerator.

YIELD: ABOUT 6 CUPS

SIMPLICITY: +

NEIMAN MARCUS BBQ SAUCE

A favorite barbecue sauce is a matter of personal taste, so I would never be so bold as to say my recipe is any better than anyone else's. A BBQ sauce recipe usually reveals where the "owner" was born and raised. Being that I'm a Yankee, I drew from my many years as a chef cooking all over the United States to create my own recipe. Whatever your fancy for a good BBQ sauce, this recipe provides a starting point.

1 tablespoon vegetable oil

2 garlic cloves, crushed

1 onion, diced

1 jalapeño, cut in half

4 cups ketchup

½ cup light brown sugar

½ cup balsamic vinegar

¼ cup honey

¼ cup dark molasses

¼ cup soy sauce

¼ cup barbecue spice (see Chef's Note)

1 tablespoon dry mustard, such as Colman's

1 tablespoon kosher salt

1 tablespoon liquid smoke (optional)

Pour the oil into a large saucepan and set over medium heat. Add the garlic, onion, and jalapeño and sauté for 3 minutes, or until softened. Add 2 cups water and the ketchup, brown sugar, vinegar, honey, molasses, soy sauce, barbecue spice, mustard, salt, and liquid smoke. Bring to a boil, then reduce the heat to low and simmer for 1 hour, until thick and flavorful. Strain into a clean container, discarding the solids. Check the seasonings and adjust as necessary.

CHEF'S NOTE: I like Head Country BBQ spice, which comes from Oklahoma. If you enjoy the smoky flavor of chipotle chiles (smoked, dried jalapeños), add ¼ cup puréed canned chipotles in adobo sauce and an additional ¼ cup honey to the finished sauce. The sauce will keep for up to 1 week in the refrigerator, and it freezes well.

YIELD: ABOUT 4 CUPS

SIMPLICITY: + +

TOMATO KETCHUP

I started making my own ketchup after growing a bumper crop of tomatoes one summer. I threw them all into a large pot and cooked them down slowly with some spices. I can't say this recipe has completely displaced the commercial brand in our home refrigerator or restaurants, but during the summer, this recipe wins hands down.

2½ pounds ripe tomatoes, cored and quartered

2 tablespoons cider vinegar

1 tablespoon light brown sugar

½ teaspoon ground ginger

¼ teaspoon garlic powder

½ teaspoon ground cloves

⅛ teaspoon cayenne pepper

Kosher salt to taste

Combine the tomatoes, vinegar, sugar, ginger, garlic powder, cloves, and cayenne in a large saucepan and bring to a simmer over medium heat. Reduce the heat to low and cook slowly for 1 hour, stirring often. Remove the pan from the heat, season with salt, and transfer the sauce to a blender. Purée the sauce and strain through a medium-fine strainer into a storage container. Let chill completely before serving.

CHEF'S NOTE: This ketchup will keep for up to 2 weeks in the refrigerator.

YIELD: ABOUT 2 CUPS

SIMPLICITY: + +

ROASTED GARLIC PURÉE

Roasting garlic mellows its sharp flavor and brings out its sweet tones. If you have never tasted garlic that has been roasted, treat your-self after making this recipe by smearing some of it over a hot piece of toasted French bread and sprinkling with a little bit of coarse salt. That something so simple can taste so heavenly is one of those miracles that makes me happy to have chosen the profession of chef.

1 large head garlic

Preheat the oven to 350°F.

Cut the garlic in half horizontally and wrap both halves in foil. Place in a small baking dish and transfer to the oven. Roast for 45 minutes. Unwrap the garlic and squeeze out the roasted cloves into a bowl. Let cool and reserve in an airtight container in the refrigerator.

CHEF'S NOTE: Store in an airtight container covered by a little olive oil; it will keep for up to 3 weeks.

YIELD: ABOUT ¼ CUP

SIMPLICITY: +

VELOUTÉ

This recipe is one of the five "mother sauces" that form the backbone of traditional French cuisine. It is made by taking a light stock (made from fish, chicken, or meat bones and vegetable scraps) and adding a roux to thicken. Serve on top of roast chicken or add grated cheese to make a cheese sauce.

2 tablespoons unsalted butter

2 tablespoons all-purpose flour

2 cups Chicken Broth (page 267) or store-bought chicken stock

¼ cup heavy cream

Kosher salt to taste

Melt the butter in a small saucepan over medium heat. Reduce the heat to low and gradually add the flour, stirring continuously with a wooden spoon. Cook for 1 minute, remove from the heat, and set aside. Pour the broth into a saucepan and bring to a boil over medium heat. Add the cream and return to a simmer. Add the flour mixture while whisking vigorously with a wire whisk, making sure there are no lumps. Bring the sauce to a simmer and cook for 4 minutes; season with salt. Strain into a clean saucepan and keep warm.

YIELD: ABOUT 2 CUPS

SIMPLICITY: + +

CRISPY CROUTONS

These tasty morsels make a wonderful garnish for soups and salads.

2 tablespoons unsalted butter

1 garlic clove, crushed

8 slices sourdough bread (crusts removed), diced

Dash of paprika

Preheat the oven to 350°F.

Melt the butter in a small saucepan over medium heat. Add the crushed garlic and heat until the butter foams, 1 to 2 minutes. Turn off the heat and add the bread cubes. Stir to mix well and then transfer the bread cubes to a cookie sheet. Sprinkle with paprika and bake in the oven for 10 minutes, or until golden brown and crisp. Remove from the oven and let cool.

YIELD: ABOUT 2 CUPS

SIMPLICITY: +

GARLIC TOAST

We use this simple recipe for Caramelized Onion Soup (page 58) and Swiss Cheese Fondue (page 88).

5 tablespoons unsalted butter

3 garlic cloves, crushed

1 French baguette loaf

Preheat the oven to 350°F.

Place the butter in a small saucepan and set over medium-low heat. Add the garlic and, when the mixture starts to sizzle, transfer it to a bowl. Cut the French loaf in half lengthwise and then again crosswise into 3-inch slices. Dip each slice of bread into the garlic-butter mixture and place on a cookie sheet. Transfer to the oven and bake for about 12 minutes, until toasted and golden brown. Serve hot.

SERVES: 8

SIMPLICITY: +

TOASTED NUTS

In the same way that roasting brings out the flavors of certain ingredients, so toasting nuts intensifies their flavor and aromatic qualities. Store toasted nuts in an airtight container.

PINE NUTS

1 cup pine nuts

Preheat the oven to 325°F.

Place the pine nuts in a single layer on a baking sheet. Transfer to the oven and toast for 10 minutes, stirring often, or until they just begin to brown. Transfer to a plate to cool; remove quickly from the baking sheet, or the nuts will continue to brown.

WALNUTS

1 cup walnut halves

Preheat the oven to 350°F.

Place the walnuts in a single layer on a baking sheet. Transfer to the oven and toast for 5 or 6 minutes, stirring often, or until they are fragrant and just beginning to brown. Transfer to a plate to cool; remove quickly from the baking sheet, or the nuts will continue to brown.

ALMONDS

1 cup sliced almonds

Preheat the oven to 325°F.

Place the almonds in a single layer on a baking sheet. Transfer to the oven and toast for about 15 minutes, stirring often, or until they are fragrant and just beginning to brown. Transfer to a plate to cool; remove quickly from the baking sheet, or the nuts will continue to brown.

ACKNOWLEDGMENTS

First off, a big thank-you to Burt Tansky, our chairman at Neiman Marcus and a consummate foodie. I met Burt when I interviewed for my current position, and I knew immediately that I wanted to work for him. I recognized his true passion for the restaurant business and appreciated the high goals he set for the world's leading retailer. I was excited to take on the challenge. With Karen Katz, our CEO, and Neva Hall, executive vice president of Neiman Marcus Stores, I have enjoyed the most rewarding partnership a chef could wish for. I tell people all the time that being the chef and vice president of restaurants at Neiman Marcus is simply the best job in the business.

Next, I have to thank my Neiman Marcus restaurant team, Frank Zack, Lynda Klempel, Jeff Dains, David Crow, and Kevin Combs, for being the best group a vice president in my position could ask for. Because they are so good at what they do, I was able to pull away from some of my daily activities to dedicate time to this cookbook. I have great confidence in this team, and they always come through with flying colors.

A huge thanks also to Anita Hirsch, my corporate chef. I have been lucky enough to have known Anita and worked with her, off and on, for more than twenty years. Anita diligently worked through the recipes in this book, making excellent comments and suggestions every step of the way. I thank her for being not only a great chef but also a trusted friend.

Two people whom I knew I could trust to keep me focused on getting this project complete and finished on time were my literary agent, David Hale Smith, a friend and big-time supporter of Neiman Marcus restaurants, and Steve Kornajcik, senior vice president of Creative Services at Neiman Marcus. Steve's keen eye for style and his calming influence are much valued. Thank you both!

Great luck struck twice for me when I was able to convince both my coauthor and my photographer from my last book, *Neiman Marcus Cookbook,* to come aboard again and see to it that this new book would become the hit the first one was. John Harrisson, my coauthor, has been the catalyst that brought each project to fruition. I am forever grateful to him for making the time, on short notice, to carefully edit every word I wrote and adding greatly to this book as it developed. Ellen Silverman, a gifted and creative photographer, happily jumped into this project with her talented group of people. Ellen's images reflect not only her exquisite eye for the perfect shot but also her skill in surrounding herself with a wonderful crew. Ellen is the first to recognize that her photographs are the result of an intensive team creative collaboration. Her assistants, Christina Holmes and Rebecca Davis, are both immensely talented in their own rights. Susan Spungeon and Susie Theodorou were responsible for styling the food for the studio shots—great job, ladies; thank you. Last but not least, Bette Blau found the props used in the studio shots, and without her, this book would never have been so beautiful.

My appreciation goes also to Rica Allannic, our editor at Clarkson Potter, whose enthusiasm and expertise were crucial in shaping the finished product, and to Pam Krauss and Marysarah Quinn. Jane Soudner and her staff at the Dallas Public Library were instrumental in helping us access archival material on Neiman Marcus history, for which I am most grateful.

I need to salute my mother, Irene, for instilling in me the principle that company is always served first. Not only did she train me in setting a beautiful table for guests but she also taught me the profound lesson that being a host is more than just cooking a great meal; it means your guests should come away with the best experience you can deliver. And she taught me that it helps to shine the silver!

Finally, I owe the biggest thank-yous of all to my wife, Jody, and son Patrick for their loving support through this entire book-writing process. Jody's comments were always accurate and to the point, and while I did not necessarily agree with her every time, I always know her taste buds are far superior to mine! Patrick was always available for taste-testing and giving me his impartial opinion, and he also did a great job at jotting down notes as I tried out the recipes at home. There's one guy who won't get to see this book— my son Josh, whom we miss every day.

NOTES ON INGREDIENTS

Unless otherwise noted: All ingredients are medium in size and fresh.

Bell peppers and **chiles** should be seeded and the internal ribs removed.

Carrots are peeled.

Flour is all-purpose and unbleached.

Garlic is peeled.

Ginger is peeled.

Milk is whole-fat (regular) milk.

Mushrooms are cleaned, if necessary, with a damp cloth or a paper towel. They should not be washed, or they may become soggy and waterlogged.

Onions are peeled.

Parsley is flat-leaf/Italian.

Pepper should always be freshly cracked (a coarse grind) or freshly ground (a fine grind). I like to use white pepper rather than black when the recipe is light in color. By using white pepper, you won't see it, but you will get a pleasant heat.

Salt should be kosher, but coarse sea salt can be substituted.

Shallots are peeled.

Sugar is white and granulated.

INGREDIENTS, TERMS, AND DEFINITIONS

CUTTING INGREDIENTS:
CHOPPING, DICING, AND
MINCING

Roughly chopped refers to ingredients that are cut into bite-size pieces (about 1½-inch cubes). These are called for in recipes where the ingredients will be puréed or discarded.

Chopped (approximately 1-inch cubes) also describes ingredients that will be removed or strained from a recipe, or puréed, such as vegetables used in a sauce for flavoring.

Large dice (¾-inch cubes) are more finely cut than chopped ones, but less fine than minced (see below). Diced ingredients, requiring more effort to be *neatly* cut, are usually part of the final presentation of a recipe.

Dice (the same as medium dice) refers to ingredients cut into ½-inch cubes. Diced ingredients are usually left in the recipe and so should be *neatly* cut.

Finely diced refers to ingredients cut *neatly* into ¼-inch cubes.

Minced or **finely minced** refers to ingredients cut smaller than ¼-inch dice, or as finely as possible; garlic and fresh herbs are examples of ingredients that are typically minced.

A Note on Mincing Fresh Italian Parsley

After mincing parsley, place it in a cloth or a kitchen towel and secure tightly. Rinse the cloth under cold running water while gently squeezing the parsley; the water will drain green. Remove the cloth from the water after 20 seconds of rinsing and gently squeeze the parsley dry. This technique helps prevent minced parsley from clumping, making it easier to sprinkle.

Notes on Preparing Ingredients

Wash raw fish, meat, and poultry in the sink and then pat dry with paper towels. Transfer to a chopping board, a work surface, or a clean plate away from the sink. Clean the board and sink thoroughly after transferring the meat to a cooking pan. Rinse or scrub potatoes and other fruits and vegetables that are not peeled. Wash salad greens, leafy greens, and herbs well before draining and drying.

Notes on Letting Cooked Foods Cool

I always let my oven-baked or roasted recipes cool a bit before serving. This hiatus lets the fibers in the roasted meats relax and become even more tender. In the case of breads, pastries, and desserts, the glutens in the flour relax to become more tender also. With casseroles, you want to allow cooling time so the liquids can settle a little after simmering. The result is a more cohesive and less runny dish.

INDEX